Praise for Supervising and Supporting Ministry Staff

"As someone who has supervised staff in multiple ministry contexts for more than thirty years, I wish I'd had a resource like Supervising and Supporting Ministry Staff available to me twenty years ago! Drawing on years of deep experience and rich research, Kevin Lawson and Mick Boersma have written an extremely insightful and practical book to guide those who are charged with supervising ministry staff. Particularly helpful are the many excerpts of interviews with both staff members and supervisors sprinkled throughout the book. Not only do I highly recommend this important book, I will be using it to personally improve my own supervision of staff."

—**Sam Rima**, lead pastor, North Seattle Church; author of
Overcoming the Dark Side of Leadership

"Biblical stewardship requires a thoughtful and intentional use of God's resources. For those who are serving as the church's shepherds, it is particularly sobering to realize that the staff members who come under our care are precious members of Christ's body and should be treated with the utmost consideration. Lawson and Boersma have provided ministry leaders with a valuable and insightful resource to help us steward the colleagues that God has entrusted to our care. This book is a must read for anyone that is supervising and nurturing ministry leaders—whether it be in the local church or in para-church ministries."

—**Michael J. Anthony**, president, Calibrate Global Consulting

Supervising and Supporting Ministry Staff

A Guide to Thriving Together

Kevin E. Lawson and Mick Boersma

An Alban Institute Book

ROWMAN & LITTLEFIELD
Lanham • Boulder • New York • London

Published by Rowman & Littlefield
A wholly owned subsidiary of
The Rowman & Littlefield Publishing Group, Inc.
4501 Forbes Boulevard, Suite 200, Lanham, Maryland 20706
https://rowman.com

Unit A, Whitacre Mews, 26-34 Stannary Street, London SE11 4AB,
United Kingdom

British Library Cataloguing in Publication Information Available

Library of Congress Cataloging-in-Publication Data

Names: Lawson, Kevin E. (Kevin Ethan), 1956- author.
Title: Supervising and supporting ministry staff : a guide to thriving
 together / Kevin E. Lawson and Mick Boersma.
Description: Lanham : Rowman & Littlefield Publishers, 2017. | "An Alban
 Institute book." | Includes bibliographical references and index.
Identifiers: LCCN 2017004180 (print) | LCCN 2017019604 (ebook) | ISBN
 9781566997874 (Electronic) | ISBN 9781566997850 (cloth : alk. paper) |
 ISBN 9781566997867 (pbk. : alk. paper)
Subjects: LCSH: Church personnel management. | Christian leadership.
Classification: LCC BV652.13 (ebook) | LCC BV652.13 .L39 2017 (print) | DDC
 254--dc23
LC record available at https://lccn.loc.gov/2017004180

Printed in the United States of America

This book is dedicated to all those faithful servants of Jesus Christ who supervise and encourage their colleagues in various ministries around the world. Whether it be the local church, para church, missions, or other manifestations of God's work, it is our hope this effort will provide guidance, encouragement, and greater effectiveness and joy to all who so labor to God's glory.

Contents

Contents

Acknowledgments

Any worthwhile endeavor depends upon the generous support of family, colleagues, and friends. The two of us are first and foremost grateful for the enthusiastic and constant support of our wives. Their enduring love and encouragement helped guide us through the challenging process of research and writing. In addition, we are thankful for Kevin's son, Nathan, who transcribed numerous interviews with precision and clarity, in spite of the dubious quality of some of our self-produced recordings. As well, Mick's wife, Rolane, provided accurate accessibility to the many pastoral supervisors' contact information, thus facilitating the wide range of our research sample.

Our colleagues here at Talbot School of Theology provided helpful insights, ideas, and feedback as we worked through this project. Their continual affirmation has been a hallmark of our many years serving in this amazing school. This includes our deans, Dr. Clint Arnold and Dr. Scott Rae, whose yearly stipends to encourage research and writing do not go unappreciated.

Then there are the current and former associate staff members, and the supervising pastors who selflessly participated in our project. Whether by online survey or face-to-face interview, they demonstrated their commitment to excellence in ministry and in helping us understand best practices in supervision and support of ministry colleagues. Together with the encouragement and resources of Rowman & Littlefield, we are pleased to present this resource toward the health and success of ministry supervisors and their staff.

Chapter One

Introduction

Foundations for Supervising and Supporting Associate Staff

Kevin E. Lawson

THE CHALLENGES OF BECOMING A
SUPERVISOR OF OTHERS IN MINISTRY

We're excited that you chose to read this book on ministry supervision. It shows that you want to invest well in the ministry efforts of your associate staff members. To help us get off to a good start, let's begin with a look at three different people and their journeys into supervising others in church staff positions and see if you can identify with one or more of them.

Stan graduated from seminary with a strong sense of calling to serve a local congregation as their pastor. He loved people, and he loved preaching, and he had a desire to see people grow in their relationship with God and live faithfully as salt and light in the world. Stan was hired by a small church in a nearby city, and he poured himself into his ministry there. Over time, God blessed that church and it grew, attracting interest from many in the community who saw a very powerful, positive witness from the members of the congregation. As the church grew, ministry demands grew as well, reaching a point where Stan and the members of the church could no longer handle them without some additional assistance. Eventually, they decided to hire another staff member to work with Stan to address their ministry needs. At first, Stan was relieved to think that he would have additional help, but then questions and doubts began to stir up within him. He knew how to do his own ministry well, and he had never really aspired to supervise other church staff in their ministry areas. Would he be good at this? How was his ministry about to change? What would it take to grow into this new ministry role?

Rachel began attending Redeemer Church while she was in college for her education degree. After graduation, she stayed in the community and taught in a local school. She also began to serve in the youth ministry at the church, and over time took on more and more responsibility. Her ministry with the youth was effective, she helped with the recruitment and training of others to assist with the youth ministry, and she became sought after to help with major events in the life of this growing church. Eventually she was hired on as the junior high ministry director, and the ministry flourished under her leadership. One day her pastor approached her and asked if she would be willing to take on a larger role at the church, leading the church's ministries with youth in grades five to twelve, which would involve supervising two other staff members. Rachel agreed to do this, but immediately began to wonder how her relationship with her ministry colleagues was about to change, and what it would mean to now be supervising others in ministry leadership roles. While she felt this change was right to pursue, it made her a little uncomfortable.

Allen was a businessman in a growing company. He had risen up through the ranks to a significant leadership role, with responsibility for a major division of the company and eight direct reports. He enjoyed his work and generally had good relationships with those he supervised. Allen was also a very active member of his church, serving as chairman of the elder board for several years. The church had also seen a significant season of growth, adding on additional staff members to serve the church in areas of worship, children's ministry, youth ministry, and missions. There had been many growing pains at the church, and it was becoming increasingly clear that there was a need to hire an executive pastor to come alongside the preaching pastor and help coordinate and support the work of the other church staff members. In a conversation over lunch with the pastor and a few elder board members, Allen was asked if he would consider coming onto the church staff as the new executive pastor. After much prayer and discussion with his wife and close friends, Allen agreed to take on this new role, feeling that God was leading him into this new ministry opportunity. As he began meeting with the different church staff members to get to know them and their ministry areas better, he also began to wonder if supervising others in a church setting would be different from what he was used to doing at his business. Certainly, some aspects must be the same, but what might he need to rethink? What supervision practices would still be appropriate and effective? What new dynamics might there be in supervising his "brothers" and "sisters" in ministering to God's people?

Three different people, all moving into roles of supervising other church staff members in their ministries. Stan is like many seminary graduates, with a heart for ministry and desire to serve well, but not necessarily planning to serve in a setting where they have to supervise other church staff. Their own ministry excites and energizes them, but taking responsibility to supervise others feels like a shift into something less comfortable, possibly less fulfilling. Rachel is like many people who start out in associate staff roles, content like Stan to do their own ministry, but finding over time that they are growing into positions of greater responsibility, including supervising others in ministry, even some who may have been their colleagues in the past. Taking on more responsibility may feel good, but the new role brings with it many new questions. Allen is like many who have excellent leadership experience outside the church setting who are called on to bring those gifts and abilities to bear within the church. They have learned a lot of good supervision practices that fit well within the business sector, but wonder if they all fit as well in the church. After all, the church is a relational community with Christ as the head, not just an organization. How does this impact their role and practices as a supervisor? How will they need to change what has worked well for them in the past?

These stories illustrate how many ministry leaders come to find themselves in supervision roles over other church staff members. You may identify with one or more of them, or you may have been in your supervisory role for many years already but still wondering if you are adequately attending to all you should as you oversee your ministry associates. We believe that these kinds of questions and concerns are both common and natural. Supervising others in their work in general has its challenges, and doing so in the church setting has its own unique aspects. This needs careful attention by those who step into these roles.

We've pursued our research and writing on these issues because we believe that when church staff members learn to work well together, in support of one another in the various ministry areas God has called them to, the church benefits, and staff members will in turn find great satisfaction in their ministry contributions. A key part of making this a reality is in how ministry supervisors both supervise and support those under their oversight. They are in a critical role to help associate staff members have fruitful ministries and thrive in the process. Let me explain with a simple analogy.

LEARNING TO SEE WITH BIFOCAL VISION

When I was in my mid-fifties, I finally gave in, swallowed my pride, and went for an eye exam. For years I had needed glasses ("cheaters") for reading and working on my computer, but now I found that even my distance vision was getting a bit blurry. I could not continue on without some help with my vision. While it was tempting to get one pair of glasses for distance vision and another for reading, I decided instead that I would get bifocals. I was officially becoming a "late-middle-aged" adult.

When my glasses arrived, I went to the store to pick them up, put them on, and then found I was having trouble walking. I had to adjust to looking through the two different lenses in my glasses, and it took a bit of practice to get used to how much I needed to tilt my head to see where my feet were going. It wasn't easy paying attention to both the near and far fields, and it took me some time to adjust to the point where it began to feel more natural and easier to shift my vision as needed. Now, after a few years, it feels quite normal. I don't even notice it.

Mick and I have frequently used this image of bifocal lenses to help us think about the responsibilities and opportunities of serving as a supervisor of others in ministry roles. Others writing in the field of leadership have described the supervision of others as having both a "task component" and a "relationship component." We agree, and this is at the heart of our understanding of the bifocal lenses image. Let me explain this image, as it is foundational to our approach throughout this book.

Lens One: Focusing on Ensuring That the Ministry Is Done Well

The reason why the church hires an associate staff member is that there is an important aspect of ministry that needs more attention than what the pastor or the congregational members can give attention to. There is a task to be done, and the anticipation is that the person hired will be able to lead the church in addressing that ministry area well. Whether it is a youth pastor, worship leader, children's pastor, family ministry leader, or other ministry associate, he or she has been hired to both lead and serve to ensure that particular ministry needs are attended to. As a supervisor of that staff member, it is natural that one of the important lenses you look through is focused on whether or not the ministry responsibilities entrusted to your staff member are satisfactorily addressed. That is why this person was hired and entrusted with their ministry areas.

When I think about my growing need for glasses, I first just needed help with close-up vision. I could see well at a distance, but glasses helped me better see things that were up close. I tend to think of focusing on the ministry tasks that need to be done as the close-up vision. It is what is right in front of us, close by. The many ministry tasks we take up each day fill our field of vision, and it can be easy to be absorbed in the immediate tasks of ministry because they are so close, needing attention. It can be very natural for ministry supervisors to see through this lens much of the time, trying to ensure that the ministry is going well. When I think about the work of the supervisor, this is what I would call "supervision proper."

Lens Two: Focusing on the Well-Being of Those Doing the Ministry

However, one of the things we can sometimes overlook is that long term, the effectiveness of ministry by church staff members flows out of their well-being, their healthy growth on the job, their ability to balance ministry demands with other aspects of life. Even when someone feels a strong sense of calling to serve in vocational ministry, the demands they face can be draining, stressful, sometimes discouraging. There are joys in ministry and seasons of great encouragement and satisfaction, and other seasons where it can be hard to find a sense of satisfaction due to ongoing challenges and exhaustion. Supervisors need to be attentive to the well-being of those they oversee, looking for ways to build them up, ensure they are getting the support they need, and helping them see the good fruit of their ministry investment. Experiencing prolonged seasons of stress can lead to burnout, turnover of staff, and disruption in the ministry. That is neither good for the ministry staff nor for the church.

When I think about my deteriorating vision and the need to finally get some glasses, I tend to think of focusing on the well-being of associate staff members as the far vision. It is the "longer view" of ministry, and of our ministry associates. It does not just focus on the immediate needs in front of us (the tasks), but also on the long-term ministry of the church staff. We can all handle short seasons of heavy work demands and stress, but if this becomes the long-term norm, it is a recipe for ministry deterioration. This lens is important for long-term ministry and health. When I think about the work of the supervisor, this is what I would call "support."

Learning to See Out of Both Lenses: Bifocal Vision

The task of ministry supervision then consists of these two equally important areas: supervision proper and the support of those who serve. From literature in the field of leadership, one basic thing we learn is that while both of these aspects of supervision are important, supervisors may find that one of these two lenses is their more natural way to approach their supervision task. It's not always a matter of not understanding the need for both lenses, but for a variety of reasons, we focus on one more than the other.

Some of us gravitate to looking through the "task" or "supervision proper" lens most of the time. After all, the ministry is important, God has called us to serve in leadership roles, people in the church are counting on us, and that's why we are here. But when we spend all of our time looking through this close-up lens, focusing on the tasks of ministry, we can discourage and burn out those we supervise. When there are heavy work demands or critical tasks to be done, it can be too easy for some of us to fix our attention here and be blind to how staff members are handling the stress. I know this is something I have to watch out for.

Others of us gravitate to looking through the "support" lens when it comes to supervision of our ministry associates. We are "people" oriented, with shepherd hearts, called to care for the needs of the flock. We came into vocational ministry because of our love for people, our desire to care for them well. As we work with associate staff members, we naturally focus our attention on how they are doing, looking for ways to support them in both their lives and their ministry areas. As appealing as this sounds, if we spend all our time looking through this far-vision lens, focusing on staff members' well-being, we can neglect important ministry areas, overlooking staff members' incompetence or inadequate planning or leadership of others.

The task of supervision of ministry associates must bring together both lenses, the areas of supervision proper and support, to ensure both that effective ministry is being carried out and that those who serve are cared for in the process. If we find ourselves attending to one lens at the expense of the other, we have to learn how to shift and make sure both are getting adequate attention. This book has been developed with an eye on each lens. What we have found is that there are many ministry leadership books available that address beneficial practices and legal aspects of "supervision proper," but not very many that focus on the important support aspects of ministry supervision. In what follows, you will see our attempt to look through both lenses at the same time. We invite you to look with us and see what you might learn to strengthen one or both aspects of your work as a ministry supervisor.

LISTENING TO ASSOCIATE STAFF MEMBERS AND THEIR MINISTRY SUPERVISORS

Mick and I want to begin with a confession. Neither of us thinks of ourselves as highly skilled or gifted ministry supervisors. While we each have loved the ministry efforts we have been involved in, and continue to do, we each recognize limitations to our work of supervising others in ministry. I know that there are times I am too focused on the "supervision proper" lens, trying to ensure that the tasks of ministry are being done well. While I care about the well-being of those who work with me, at times I can be blind to how they are struggling. That can create real problems. Mick is such a shepherd at heart that the "support" lens comes naturally to him, but the "supervision proper" lens is more difficult to keep in focus. We both knew that if we were going to write a book like this, it could not be based just on our own experiences and ideas. We needed the help of others to better understand how to effectively attend to both the task and support aspects of supervising ministry associates.

A few years ago, we collaborated in some research on what helps associate staff members thrive in ministry. Our book, *Associate Staff Ministry: Thriving Personally, Professionally, and Relationally* (2014, Rowman & Littlefield), focused on a wide range of commitments and practices that help associate staff members navigate the challenges of ministry and thrive long term. One of the most critical aspects we heard about repeatedly from the associate staff members we studied was about the important things their ministry supervisors did that helped them thrive. We learned a lot from these associate staff members and some of what we learned is reflected in this book. We also came away from that experience with a desire to learn more, to spend time with some exemplary supervising pastors and listen to their reflections on what it takes to supervise associate staff members well. We wanted to see what we could learn that we could pass on to others in these roles for their sake, and the sake of their ministry associates. After that first book was published, we began our research on supervising associate staff well.

The first phase of our study was to contact people who currently serve or who had recently served in associate staff roles to ask them four basic questions about their experiences with their supervisors. These questions addressed four areas, including: what their supervisors had done to help them serve in their ministry areas and grow in their ability to do it well; what their supervisors had done that helped them feel personally supported in their ministry efforts; what their supervisors had done that made it difficult to serve well in their areas of ministry; and what their supervisors had done that made them not feel supported in their work. About 150 current and former associate staff members responded to our survey and provided reflections on their experiences with their ministry supervisors. More details on this part of the study are available in appendix B of this book.

In addition to asking for their responses to the questions noted above, we also explained that we were looking to interview exemplary ministry supervisors. We invited those who had a particularly good ministry supervisor to e-mail us with that person's name and contact information so we could ask to interview him or her about his or her perspectives and practices as a supervisor. About twenty supervisors were identified this way, and we were able to arrange interviews with sixteen of them. We either met at a restaurant and carried out the interview over lunch or sometimes did the interviews by conference phone call. The focus of our interviews was on how they approached their roles as supervisors, what they had found beneficial to do as a supervisor and why, and what they would pass on to other ministry staff supervisors about helping associate staff thrive in their ministries. A description of that interview process, and how the data from the surveys and interviews were analyzed, is described in appendix B of this book.

SOME FOUNDATIONAL PRINCIPLES FROM SCRIPTURE FOR SUPERVISING ASSOCIATE STAFF IN MINISTRY

In addition to this research data, there are a few foundational principles from Scripture that have shaped our understanding and vision of supervising others in ministry. These also serve as a guide to what we write about, so it is good to take a closer look at them before we get into our findings. These principles are not the only ones that we think are relevant from Scripture for issues of ministry supervision, but they are key foundational cornerstones we feel compelled to identify up front and build upon.

We are "undershepherds" together under the Great Shepherd. Leadership in the church is meant to be exercised by a plurality of leaders, or elders. This fits well with the idea of multiple-staff ministry. This leadership, in whichever areas a staff member serves, is to be exercised as "shepherding," caring for the needs of the flock, not seeking our own gain. 1 Peter 5:1–4 states:

> I exhort the elders among you, as a fellow elder . . . shepherd the flock of God that is among you, exercising oversight, not under compulsion, but willingly, as God would have you; not for shameful gain, but eagerly; not domineering over those in your charge, but being examples to the flock. And when the chief Shepherd appears, you will receive the unfading crown of glory.

Our ministry together is for the sake of God's flock, God's people, and we do so to please God, not ourselves. God is the true "Shepherd" of the church, not us, and we need to continually see ourselves as "undershepherds," serving under God's supervision. Ministry supervisors understand this, model it, and encourage their associate staff members toward a similar vision.

We serve out of God's grace and faithfulness to us. None of us is clever enough, smart enough, wise enough, gifted enough, skilled enough, or good enough on our own to have earned the right to lead God's people or to supervise others in ministry roles. We all first receive God's grace and calling to serve, and then we continually draw on God's grace and faithfulness to make us adequate for what God calls us to do in ministry. In 1 Timothy 1, Paul, one of the most highly recognized leaders of the early church, shares how he had received mercy and grace from God that led to his growth in faith and love for God. In verses 15 and 16 he then says:

> The saying is trustworthy and deserving of full acceptance, that Christ Jesus came into the world to save sinners, of whom I am the foremost. But I received mercy for this reason, that in me, as the foremost, Jesus Christ might display his perfect patience as an example to those who were to believe in him for eternal life.

This important reminder moves us to humility in our work together, recognizing that each of us may sin and fail at times, but by God's grace we can be restored to God's use, and we can serve together because we have all received, and continue to receive, God's mercy and grace. Ministry leaders model this themselves, and it shows in how they treat their ministry associates who, like themselves, are less than perfect.

We are family first, not just leaders of an organization. One of the most prevalent images in Scripture for the church is "family." Family relational images permeate the New Testament, calling us God's "household, bride, and adopted children." In our relationships with one another in the church, we are called "brothers" and "sisters." We are not just some volunteer organization that attracts like-minded people. As God's adopted children, we are remade into God's family and expected to live accordingly. In 1 John 3:16–18 we read:

> By this we know love, that he laid down his life for us, and we ought to lay down our lives for the brothers. But if anyone has the world's goods and sees his brother in need, yet closes his heart against him, how does God's love abide in him? Little children, let us not love in word and talk but in deed and in truth.

There is no excuse for treating other congregation members better than we do one another on church staff. In fact, the many "one anothers" in Scripture (e.g., love, accept, forgive, pray for, admonish, encourage, bear with, build up) apply to our work relationships as much as they do to those with members of the church. A radical love for one another, even if there are hard things to be faced and worked through, must characterize our relationships together on staff. Ministry supervisors relentlessly pursue and reinforce these kinds of relationships with and among their associate staff members.

We serve together with diverse gifts, but are united with a common identity and calling. Another prominent image for the church in Scripture is the "body" imagery with its emphasis on diverse spiritual gifts and areas of service, but unity under the headship of Christ Jesus. 1 Corinthians 12:4–7 reminds us:

> Now there are varieties of gifts, but the same Spirit; and there are varieties of service, but the same Lord; and there are varieties of activities, but it is the same God who empowers them all in everyone. To each is given the manifestation of the Spirit for the common good.

This image emphasizes our unity and mutual dependence, and the value of what each of us contributes as we exercise the differing gifts and callings God has given us to serve the church. We are called to cooperate with each other as we serve, valuing what each of us is able to contribute to the body.

There is no room for ministry silos or "kingdoms" that function in competition with other ministry areas of the church. We are one body, and we need one ministry team serving together, supporting and valuing one another. Ministry supervisors strive to ensure this is lived out in their ministry team of staff members.

We are called to be means of grace to one another. In 1 Peter 4:10–12, in light of Christ's coming return, Peter exhorts us with these words:

> As each has received a gift, use it to serve one another, as good stewards of God's varied grace: whoever speaks, as one who speaks oracles of God; whoever serves, as one who serves by the strength that God supplies—in order that in everything God may be glorified in Jesus Christ. To him belong glory and dominion forever and ever. Amen.

We are meant to be means of grace to one another, and to receive God's grace through one another. We must learn to see each other as channels of God's grace to us, and to the church. When we serve one another in our ministry leadership roles, with the different gifts God has given us, we receive God's grace through each other, and God is the one who is glorified. We don't pursue ministry leadership roles so that we will be well thought of or affirmed, but so that God will be glorified through Jesus Christ. Ministry supervisors are open to the grace of God coming through those they supervise and encourage all staff to use their gifts to glorify God through their ministries.

A ROAD MAP TO THIS BOOK AND HOW TO USE IT

With this foundation laid, over the next eight chapters, we will share what we have learned about best supervision practices that address both the "near lens" of the task of ministry, and the "far lens" of the support of those you supervise in ministry. We will address key issues and practices, provide quotes from supervisors and associate staff alike, and at the end of each chapter offer a few questions for your own reflection, and some for possible discussion with those you supervise. We trust that as you work through this material, if you take time to reflect and discuss what you read, it can lead you to strengthened supervision practices and a stronger sense of unity and support in ministry together.

We begin in chapter 2 with some basics on forming and leading a ministry team. There has been a lot of research on what helps groups of people work well together as a team. We take some of that research and then look at how this plays out on a ministry staff in a church context. Much of what we discuss in this chapter is foundational to the chapters that follow.

In chapters 3 and 4, we explore three different kinds of meetings and group gatherings and how to use them well for clarification of communication, planning, review, encouragement, correction, learning together, and so on. Chapter 3 focuses on one of the important foundational practices: how to have constructive regular team meetings (RTMs). Beyond the RTM, chapter 4 addresses four different kinds of occasional team gatherings (i.e., spiritual retreats, planning retreats, conferences and seminars, socials and celebrations) and how to have regular productive one-on-one meetings with those you supervise.

In chapter 5, we look primarily through the "task" lens to understand what a supervisor can do to facilitate and support the ministry of their associate staff members. What is your role in ensuring that they are equipped and able to tackle the responsibilities they have been entrusted with? Some supervisors try to simply delegate ministry and end up neglecting their associate staff, hindering the effectiveness of their ministries. You have a critical role to play, even when you are not "hands on" in their ministry area.

We shift our focus in chapter 6, looking through the "support" lens to explore ways you can support and provide a healthy ministry environment for the staff members you supervise. Much of their sense of satisfaction in ministry can be enhanced through the ways you foster spiritual, family, and professional support for them. You have an opportunity to minister to them, encourage them, and help them persevere through the challenges that come with ministry leadership.

One of the critical areas that needs to be done well to help staff members be affirmed in their work, and help them grow in ministry effectiveness, is staff reviews. Chapter 7 addresses beneficial staff review practices and ways to provide opportunities for staff development on the job. We all have areas to grow in, and good supervisors look for ways to help their staff grow to meet the needs of a growing ministry.

As ministry progresses, situations may come up where it would seem best to a staff member, or to a ministry supervisor, for a staff member to transition into another ministry, either at the church or in another setting. Chapter 8 addresses how to have a positive transition process, bringing grace to bear in situations where it becomes clear that there is a need for a change.

Finally, in chapter 9, we turn our attention to you, the ministry supervisor, and to important practices to help ensure that you have a healthy ministry life. Your leadership and ministry with your associate staff members flows out of your own thriving in ministry. We want to help you be attentive to your own health and vitality as you serve. This is important for your own ministry and also provides a strong model and support for your associate staff members to attend to their own health as well.

TAKING INVENTORY

As I shared above, at the end of each chapter, we will provide some questions on the issues raised in the chapter for your personal reflection, and some for possible discussion with the staff members you supervise. We would not expect or recommend that you try to answer all of the questions at the end of each chapter, but select the topic areas that seem most in need of reflection and discussion with your supervisees, and spend time working through them.

For this first chapter, here are some initial questions just for your reflection.

1. What was your vocational path to your current role as a supervisor of others in ministry? What experiences do you think prepared you well for this?

2. If you once served as an associate staff member yourself, what did you most appreciate from your ministry supervisor? Were there practices you have adopted yourself?

3. If you once served as an associate staff member yourself, what did your supervisor do that made your ministry more challenging or discouraging? Are there practices you are trying to avoid?

4. Which of the "lenses" do you think you tend to look through more often, and more naturally: supervision proper (task) or support? How do you think your associate staff members would answer this question about you?

5. What are your own foundational Scriptural principles that guide your approach to supervising others in ministry? Do the ones we mentioned fit your approach to some degree? What other ones are important to you?

6. What challenges of supervision are you most hoping will be addressed in this book?

Chapter Two

Forming and Leading the Ministry Team

Kevin E. Lawson

"I DON'T KNOW WHAT YOU MEAN"

Fresh out of seminary, I became an associate staff member at a growing church in the Midwest. There were three of us on pastoral staff, led by a very gifted preacher. We each had our areas of responsibility, and I worked hard to fit in to this new congregation; oversee my ministry areas; and recruit, train, and supervise lay ministry leaders. I was new to vocational ministry and needed some mentoring, but over time, it seemed that the pastoral staff were all running on different tracks and there was little support for each other's work, or collaboration in what we were doing. At one point, I expressed to my supervising pastor that I wished we could work together more as a team. He responded with, "I don't know what you mean." The problem was, I did not know what I meant either, at least I could not put into words what I longed for and felt was missing. Over the years, I have continued to reflect on this and explore church-staff work dynamics and how to create healthy teamwork environments. I confess that my understanding is sometimes ahead of my own practice, and this is not an easy thing to maintain over time, but associate staff members in our research and the supervisors we interviewed all talked about how important this was and shared some practices that help make it possible. Here is one example from a supervising pastor of what it was like to have no sense of teamwork on the staff as an associate staff member.

> *I was part of a church staff that was not a team, and the pastor . . . said, "I love the Bible, I like to teach, but I really don't like people that much, and I wish I never had to deal with people." And that bled over to how he related to*

the staff, and the mentality was basically you're doing your job if I don't have
to hear about any problems. So do your job, don't mess up, and if I don't have
to hear about it, I'm happy. And it was just sad.

On a more positive note, others commented on how beneficial it was to them
when there was a strong culture of teamwork. One supervisor reflected on his
own experience as an associate staff member and the impact of feeling part
of a team in ministry.

> *. . . he really went out of his way to make sure that everybody felt like they*
> *were part of the team and everyone's role mattered. Like what you did mat-*
> *tered to the Kingdom and to the church, and then there was this sense of*
> *"You're here because I believe in you, and I'm believing God to do great*
> *things through you." And it was just a wonderful experience feeling like,*
> *"Hey, I'm part of something. I'm highly valued, and what I'm doing is signifi-*
> *cant to the overall mission of the church."*

In many ways, the issues surrounding this concept of teamwork are foundational to thriving together in ministry and help set the framework for this
book. Let's take a closer look at these popular, yet fuzzy, ideas of teams and
teamwork.

TEAMS AND TEAMWORK IN MINISTRY[1]

In American culture, we love teams and the idea of teamwork. We love our
sports teams and enjoy watching athletes work together to achieve their goals
(generally, beating another team). In most cases, we love the egalitarian spirit
of teamwork and resist a hierarchical approach in our work environments.
But even with sports teams, there are differing levels of "teamwork." For
example, in some sports, like rowing, teammates all do the same thing at the
same time ("stroke, stroke"), and if they get out of sync with each other they
flounder. In other sports, like basketball or football, teammates have different
roles, yet they work together in highly coordinated ways to get the ball down
the court or field to score points. In still other sports, like gymnastics or golf,
there may be a team, but each member is responsible to play his or her own
game. They may collaborate in training and share advice on how to deal with
different hazards, but in the end, it is the cumulative score of each player's
round that counts. They may function differently as teams, yet in each case
there is some measure of teamwork needed and valued.

Seeing the differences in teamwork in various sports can help us begin to
understand the range of ways that church staff members can work together,
support one another, and together accomplish their ministry goals in pursuit
of the mission of their congregations. Our work together may at times be
more integrated and synchronized, like when we collaborate to pull off a

church-wide emphasis on missions. At other times, we may each be "playing our own game" as we lead our ministry areas, yet we can learn from each other and support each other in our overarching pursuit of God's purposes for our church.

When researchers on teams and teamwork define what they mean by teams, they say things like:

> A team is a small number of people with complementary skills who are committed to a common purpose, performance goals, and approach for which they hold themselves mutually accountable. [2]

Some parts of this definition seem to fit church staff situations well. We often have a small number of people with complementary skills, and we are committed to a common purpose overall. Yet, due to the different demands of our ministry areas, we often have different performance goals and ministry approaches. Jon Katzenbach and Douglas Smith, longtime researchers on teams and effective workgroups, recognize this and make a distinction in their book, *The Wisdom of Teams*, between the group disciplines needed in "real teams" and the fundamentals of effective groups that apply to all work groups, even if they are not "real teams." In other words, we may not always be functioning in a highly coordinated "real team" way, but we always need to pursue good "teamwork" together. Let's examine some of the fundamentals of effective teamwork and how they apply to ministry teams of church staff members.

WHAT CONTRIBUTES TO EFFECTIVE TEAMWORK

I think we all have some sense of what helps people work well together and what makes it difficult. From our own experience, we can identify many things that have helped the work groups we have been a part of function well. This is also an area that has received a lot of attention in a variety of work situations, leading to some solid research on characteristics and practices of effective teamwork. I'm going to review some of what has been learned that I think fits well in church staff work situations.

Katzenbach and Smith, in *The Discipline of Teams*,[3] a follow-up to their earlier book, identify five fundamentals for effective group functioning, all of which seem relevant for church staffs seeking to work well together, even if each person has different areas of ministry responsibility.

Clear Charter/Purpose: "The group has or develops an understandable charter that provides the group with a reason and purpose for working together." Other authors call this a "clear and elevating goal."[4] A clear and meaningful sense of purpose helps us develop unity in our commitment together in ministry.

Open Communication: "Members of the group communicate and coordinate effectively to allow constructive interactions involving all of the members." Because we have different tasks on church staff, there is a need to communicate well what is happening in our ministry areas, what we are pursuing, what help is needed, and then together figure out how to coordinate our efforts well.

Clear Roles and Responsibilities: "Members of the group establish clear roles and areas of responsibility, which allow them to work individually or collectively." Clarity in our roles and responsibilities is critical for understanding where we need to coordinate well with others and where we have ministry initiatives to pursue on our own. Clarity is a foundation for confidence.

Efficient Group Processes: "Members create a time-efficient process, minimizing wandering discussions and wasted time." Knowing that there are some aspects of our work that need coordination, systems of communication and collaboration must be developed and consistently used to facilitate both the group work and the individual work of each staff member.

Assessment and Accountability: "The group develops a sense of accountability, helping each member understand individual contributions to the success of the group; hence, progress can be monitored and evaluated accordingly."

Anyone who has worked in groups for very long can testify to the importance of these five areas. Much of what goes well in our work together is tied to these five things, and much of what goes wrong relates to one or more of them. What is the role of supervising pastors in facilitating these important aspects of a group's work together?

HOW TEAM LEADERS PROMOTE TEAM EFFECTIVENESS

It appears that many of these five "fundamentals" are things that team leaders, such as supervising pastors, play a key role in establishing and maintaining. Another pair of researchers, Frank LaFasto and Carl Larson, in *When Teams Work Best*,[5] a follow-up to their earlier *Teamwork* book, specifically focused on what it is that good team leaders do that promotes team effectiveness. After studying over six thousand team members and leaders, they identified six dimensions of team leadership that make a significant difference to team performance. These include:

Maintaining the Team's Goals: Team leaders help their teams focus on the goal by keeping it clear and avoiding politics. In addition, leaders help each team member see his or her relevance to the accomplishment of the goal. Finally, leaders revisit and renew the group's understanding and commitment to the goal over time.

Fostering Collaboration and Communication: Team leaders ensure a collaborative climate by fostering safe and open communication and not tolerating it when this is violated. They reward collaborative behavior instead of competition, guide problem-solving efforts, and suppress their own egos to help the team achieve its goal. Clear and open communication builds trust and confidence.

Keeping a Positive Focus: Team leaders build confidence by their positive attitude, getting small results and affirming them, keeping the team informed of progress, showing trust in delegation to others, and accentuating the positive within the group. There may be challenges, but the leader focuses on the opportunities and each step of progress toward the goal, and they help team members do the same.

Providing Technical Help: Team leaders demonstrate sufficient technical know-how for their own role and get help where they need it—many times from other members of the team. They also help team members get the help they need when they run into demands beyond their skill set, without feeling a sense of failure.

Prioritizing among Tasks: When there is much to be done (and that seems to always be true in church ministry), team leaders set priorities for the team members and do not dilute the group's energy with too many efforts, helping them avoid being overwhelmed or discouraged. They update the team members on changes in priorities as needed.

Giving Performance Feedback: Team leaders manage performance of team members and address problems when someone is not doing his or her job. They work with team members to set specific objectives, follow up with assessment, give constructive feedback, help with personal and professional development, and reward results.

PRIORITIES AND PRACTICES FOR TEAMWORK TOGETHER WITH ASSOCIATE STAFF

With the research of Katzenbach and Smith and Larson and LaFasto as a foundation, and in light of what the associate staff members and supervising pastors in our research have shared with us, there seems to be much that a supervising pastor can do to foster a healthy and effective teamwork environment with associate staff members. We've identified ten critical areas for your reflection and attention (table 2.1) and shared some practical ways they can be pursued. As you read through, thank God for those areas that are going well, and consider if there are any that could use some focused effort to strengthen them. I'll share some reflection questions at the end that may be helpful.

Table 2.1.   Ten Priorities and Practices for Teamwork Together

Maintaining clear goals and fostering unified commitment

Clarifying roles, responsibilities, procedures, and processes

Keeping communication open and clear

Developing a collaborative climate

Drawing on others' strengths

Setting and communicating priorities

Establishing standards of excellence

Building team morale over time

Fostering external support—in the church and from God

Assessing and developing team members

Maintaining Clear Goals and Fostering Unified Commitment: One of the critical tasks of a ministry group leader is to help their group members maintain focus on the goals of the ministry over time by keeping them clear and avoiding local political issues that can divert attention and energy from the main tasks. Leaders also need to help group members see the relevance of their efforts toward the accomplishment of the goals so they can find satisfaction in their service. When ministry goals are unclear, it can lead to a sense of confusion and insecurity, or conflicting goals developing in different ministry areas. Commitment to the ministry can also subside due to a lack of understanding and valuing of a commonly held goal for the group's ministry efforts. Because goals can fade over time in the stress of ministry, leaders also need to find ways to revisit and renew the goals with team members over time, sustaining a strong unified commitment within the group. This can be done through rewards and affirmation for work that contributes to goal accomplishment, periodically revisiting the needs and goals you are addressing, and celebrating small successes on the way toward the ultimate goal.

Practices that help:

- Taking time in regular meetings or special times away together to revisit the mission, purpose, and goals of the church's overall ministry, and how each ministry leader's area contributes to these overall goals.
- As new ministry initiatives are proposed, using the goal statements of your ministry to evaluate whether or not to take on the proposed ministry.
- In one-on-one meetings with team members, reviewing the importance of their ministry areas and their goals to the overall achievement of the church's purpose and goals.

- Periodic celebrations in team gatherings to affirm significant ministry achievements that fulfill the ministry goals of the church.

Practices that hinder:

- Assuming that since we discussed goals a year ago, everyone is still good and set to go.
- Assuming that everyone knows how their ministry area fits within and supports the church in accomplishing our overall goals.
- Assuming that because we have clarified our ministry goals, everyone shares the same commitment to achieving them.
- Allowing a team member's ministry area to develop without taking time to evaluate it in light of the church's overall ministry goals.

Clarifying Roles, Responsibilities, Procedures, and Processes: In light of the ministry goals, each member of the staff needs to understand his or her roles and responsibilities in the overall church ministry. Clear understanding in these areas builds confidence and frees the staff member to give full energy and attention to their aspects of the ministry. It also helps in understanding priorities and how success can be assessed and affirmed. In addition, understanding the procedures and processes within the church for carrying out ministry together is critical for reducing confusion and conflict. When staff members are unclear regarding their roles or responsibilities, it creates confusion, stress, and insecurity. Lack of understanding of important procedures and processes can lead to conflict, stress, and frustration. Team leaders make sure that each member of the staff team understands his or her roles and responsibilities and is familiar with the important procedures and processes that impact their areas of ministry.

Practices that help:

- Clearly developed job descriptions that are reviewed at least annually and adjusted as ministry responsibilities change over time.
- As a team, reviewing each team member's ministry roles and responsibilities so all understand who to interact with regarding questions in different ministry areas. This can be very important on larger staffs as roles and responsibilities evolve over time.
- Orientation for new team members regarding procedures and processes that are relevant for their ministry area, including key people to interact with about different kinds of issues.

Practices that hinder:

- Not having any written job description or list of responsibilities for team members.
- Having an old job description that is never used in the review process with staff members.
- Assuming everyone knows what everyone else is responsible for.
- Assuming everyone knows how to navigate the decision process for key aspects of their ministry areas (e.g., budgeting, requisition requests, personnel recruitment, equipment reservation).

Keeping Communication Open and Clear: An environment where open communication flourishes is essential for group members working together. Team leaders need to set the example by being good communicators and by fostering an environment where group members feel safe and will not get defensive when they need to be accountable to each other or to acknowledge when they are not meeting the team expectations. When open communication is encouraged, team members will support one another, help a team member to act, and complement one another, especially in the areas of weaknesses. Communication is expected from the leader to his or her team but is also important among group members, especially when they need to work together to define steps and actions to solve problems. Poor communication patterns erode work relationships, slow down decision making, create stress as conflicts or misunderstandings simmer over time, and can lead to isolation and mistrust. This is one of the more critical of the ten areas discussed here, and we will have a lot to say on this in our next chapter on team meetings and one-on-one interaction.

Practices that help:

- Regularly scheduled team meetings where everyone is brought up-to-date on what is happening and has the opportunity to ask questions, share ideas, give feedback.
- Regular one-on-one times with each associate staff member to hear what is happening, ask questions, debrief ministry events, problem solve if possible.
- Modeling open communication and accountability to the team as the team leader, with appropriate levels of transparency regarding challenges you face.
- Active listening that draws people out in difficult conversations.

Practices that hinder:

- Keeping most communication one-way, from the leader to the team members, without inviting feedback and questions.
- Not making group gatherings a priority to maintain communication and support for one another in their ministry areas.
- Reactions in group gatherings that make it feel unsafe to raise questions or concerns.
- Allowing unresolved conflict between team members to shut down communication.

Developing a Collaborative Climate: Team leaders build a collaborative climate by fostering safe communication within the group and not tolerating it when this is violated. Group members must not undermine the collaborative climate by their behaviors, whether in group settings or not. Good team leaders also reward collaborative behavior, guide problem-solving efforts, and suppress their own ego to help the team achieve its goal. They model what it means to deny oneself for the good of the group, to put Kingdom goals ahead of personal ones, and to lead with humility and grace. When a spirit of competition prevails in a ministry team, it leads to conflict over resources, the establishment of ministry area fiefdoms with little regard for the overall ministry of the church, and limited support across ministry areas between staff members. Team leaders need to do all they can to reduce any sense of competition for scarce resources and promote cross-ministry collaboration and support.

Practices that help:

- Public affirmation of collaborative efforts between team members.
- Private correction when team members exhibit a spirit of competition with colleagues for resources, or a lack of regard for one another's ministries.
- Encouraging team members to visit and participate in one another's ministry areas where appropriate.
- Modeling a spirit of humility in one's role and work, and sacrifice for the good of the ministry.
- Encouragement of new ministry initiatives that draw together different areas of the church's ministry (e.g., missions and youth ministry, children and worship, family ministry and outreach).

Practices that hinder:

- Systems that reward competitive behavior instead of coordination between ministry departments (e.g., scheduling church facilities or equipment, scheduling major events on the church calendar). [Note: I have my own embarrassing experience with this, where in one church I saw my worship ministry colleague as a competitor for the church buses and simply planned further ahead than he did to ensure I always had the buses for my youth events. Not my finest hour!]

- Public correction or criticism of a staff member's ideas or questions.
- Modeling a spirit of "RHIP" (rank has its privileges).
- Maintaining ministry isolation, "silos" of ministry efforts that never connect with other ministry areas in the church.

Drawing on Each Others' Strengths: Team leaders demonstrate sufficient technical know-how for their own responsibilities, but also get help from others on the team when they need it. A commitment to God's glory and His Kingdom goals, and recognizing God's gifting of others, allows a leader to not always be in charge or in control of all aspects of the work of the group. This requires humility and a passion for the achievement of the goals of the group, no matter who gets the credit. When this is modeled by the leader, it encourages others in the group to give of themselves and to use their strengths to their fullest. If leaders are insecure in their own ministry areas or gifting, this can be a challenge. Pride is a subtle temptation that ironically grows where our insecurities may be strongest. Good team leaders maintain such a strong commitment to God's Kingdom purposes that they affirm the strengths of others and allow them to grow and be exercised for the benefit of the church.

Practices that help:

- Public affirmation of the gifts of team members.
- Asking another member of the team to take the lead on something that fits their background, training, and skills.
- Sharing credit for ministry achievements, helping congregation members know about the blessing you have in your associate staff members.
- Revisiting and reaffirming the ministry purposes and goals you are all pursuing together on your team.
- Devotional time reflecting on temptations to pride, insecurities, and seeking God's help to let these go and rest in His grace.

Practices that hinder:

- Keeping public ministry opportunities, and the affirmation that comes with them, to oneself, not sharing them with associate staff members.
- Always keeping the leadership and control of the church's ministry within your own hands.

- Micromanaging other team members' ministry efforts.
- Never affirming the gifts of others on the team or drawing on their areas of expertise in your own ministry areas.

Setting and Communicating Priorities: Team leaders set priorities and do not dilute their group's energy with too many efforts. As situations change, they update their team members on changes in priorities as needed. This helps focus energy and clarify the critical goals that need to be achieved, allowing group members to determine what they need to do now and what can wait until later. When leaders allow too many goals to accumulate without differentiating their priority, they create a situation in which group members may feel overwhelmed, drained because there is no sense of accomplishment or progress. Team members can also feel frustrated that they are never sure if they are working on the right tasks. Setting priorities allows team members to focus their efforts, see progress, and have a sense of achievement as projects are completed. Time should also be taken to celebrate significant achievements, affirming the work of the group and the importance of what has been accomplished.

Practices that help:

- Regular meetings where ministry priorities are discussed and updated and permission is given to allow some ministry tasks to wait while others that are more critical are pursued.
- Clarifying with each team member if there are critical aspects of their work that need focused attention.
- Simple celebrations and affirmations of work well done, when team members have "gone the extra mile," even though there is still much to be done.
- Communicating ministry priorities to the congregation so they can appreciate and affirm the ministry efforts of the church staff members.

Practices that hinder:

- Allowing too many tasks, projects, and goals to accumulate for team members, creating a sense of being overwhelmed by the scope of the demands of ministry.
- Not having regular meetings where ministry priorities can be reviewed and revised.
- Not monitoring the workload and stress of team members, allowing them to bear the burden of too much stress for too long, leading to burnout.
- Always reviewing what needs to be done, but never celebrating what has been accomplished.

Establishing Standards of Excellence: Standards of excellence require mutual accountability, team assessment, and celebration. Team leaders need to help the team to clearly define the performance that is expected of each member. When group members know and are committed to work on their specific tasks and responsibilities, each of them will contribute to foster high performance among the team. Mutual accountability requires trusting each other and having confidence in each group member's abilities and power to make decisions. Leaders need to keep in mind that teams may not continue to be together when they accomplish the goal or specific project that brought them together; however, during the time they are working together, group members who are encouraged by their leaders become able to move from individual to mutual accountability. It is mutual accountability that makes possible team assessment, where no individual fails or succeeds but the team as a whole does. Therefore, rewards and celebration for accomplishments are focused on team accomplishments, not on individual accomplishments.

Practices that help:

- Modeling the kinds of standards of excellence in ministry that you desire from your team members.
- Taking time to clarify the standards you are aiming for in particular ministry initiatives, helping those involved to understand what they are aiming for and what qualifies as a worthy effort.
- As team members exhibit high standards for their work, affirming this publicly.
- Assess ministry efforts by the team as a whole where you can, not just individual efforts. Discuss how well you as a group did in pursuing and accomplishing particular goals. Encourage assessment by the team, not just by the leader. Affirm and celebrate group success where possible.

Practices that hinder:

- Always focusing assessment at an individual level.
- Never affirming and celebrating team accomplishments.
- Modeling a lack of concern for excellence in ministry, assuming that "this is the best we can do under the circumstances."
- Always focusing assessment on what can be better next time, without acknowledging what was done well this time.

Building Team Morale over Time: Team leaders build confidence by their positive attitude, helping the group achieve small results and affirming them, keeping the team informed of progress, showing trust by delegating important tasks to others, and accentuating the positive within the group.

Morale maintenance is not just the leader's responsibility, but it is one that must be modeled by the leader. Group members will at times be discouraged, have doubts about the ability of the group to achieve their goals, and see the problems more clearly than the opportunities. Without careful attention, team members may resign in discouragement. Team leaders help renew hope in the midst of challenges, help team members focus on God's grace and provision, and affirm and celebrate what has been accomplished, not just focus on what remains to be done.

Practices that help:

- With challenging ministry efforts, highlighting the small steps that are being done well, the small wins, and the value of the effort shown by those who are working hard.
- Modeling a positive attitude grounded in God's faithfulness.
- Helping team members see the progress, which sometimes can be overlooked due to the enormity of what needs to be done.
- Having times of praise and worship together regarding what God has done, and seeking God's help for the work that remains.

Practices that hinder:

- As described above, keeping the focus on what needs to be done, or what needs to be done better next time, without affirming significant effort and the accomplishments that have already come. Always seeing the problems that remain, not the ones that have been resolved.
- Allowing the stress and demands of the ministry to take your eyes off the God who has called you to serve.
- Keeping all important tasks to yourself, communicating your lack of confidence in your team members to exercise their gifts in ministry.
- Ignoring the discouragement of your team members, assuming that if they would just pray about their challenges, they would feel better.

Fostering External Support—in the Church and from God: Mutual support among group members is critical to accomplish the goals. However, in the context of Christian community, team leaders need to promote external support from the church as a community that cares for its staff members and their ministries. Team leaders also need to identify the resources that team members need for their ministry areas and ensure they are provided. For example: a place to meet and to work, equipment, financial resources, and people in positions of authority who will support their decision making. When responsibility is given, but not the resources to accomplish the ministry, it communicates a low value of that ministry area and creates stress and frustration for the staff member. Adequate resources for the ministry goals affirm the importance of that ministry area and affirm the staff member in his or her work. To promote congregational support for staff members in their ministry areas, celebration of ministry team accomplishments ought to take place when church members get together, creatively recognizing specific achievements by the team as part of the church's overall ministry goals. But above all, Christian leaders need to lead their teams to look for God's support as the ultimate source of power and authority. It is God who approves and prospers the work in God's Kingdom, and who can say, "Well done, good and faithful servant."

Practices that help:

- Lead your team in prayer for God's provision and the ability to be wise stewards with what God provides for your ministry efforts.
- Help team members identify the resources needed to accomplish their ministry goals and plans, and where and how they can be obtained.
- With your church boards, advocate for your team members, for the importance of their ministry areas and the resources needed to be successful in what they have been asked to do.
- Keep the congregation informed about the different ministry areas of the church, the significant impact they are having, their needs, and the efforts of those who lead them.
- Celebrate ministry accomplishments in public worship settings, encouraging congregational support for team members and their ministry areas.

Practices that hinder:

- Not keeping the congregation informed of the various ministry areas of the church or the needs their leaders face.
- Adding responsibilities onto the workloads of team members, but not adequately increasing their resources and staffing support ("make more bricks, with no straw").
- Not keeping church boards up-to-date on the various ministries of the church and their needs. Not advocating for the staff and their ministry areas.
- Not publicly affirming the ministry achievements of team members and their ministry areas.

Assessing and Developing Team Members: Team leaders need to oversee and assess the performance of team members and address problems when someone is not doing his or her job well. They help team members by setting specific objectives, giving constructive feedback, creating support for personal and professional development, and rewarding positive results. When team members know that the leader is doing this well, it allows each of them to focus on his or her own efforts, trusting that challenges in other ministry areas will be addressed, and others will be prepared to do their part as needed. When assessment is neglected, and there is no investment in helping ministry leaders grow on the job, problems can grow over time and eventually lead to a crisis of leadership. Leaders must recognize that there will always be a need to help team members develop on the job, learn new skills, try out new responsibilities, and receive feedback on how they handle new challenges. Supervision and support are two sides of the leadership coin, and formative assessment is an ongoing process that can lead to a stronger team over time. We'll have much more to say on this in chapter 6.

Practices that help:

- Having regularly scheduled times for debriefing ministry events, updates on future events, review of challenges staff members are facing, and resources and support needed.
- Having performance reviews at least annually, allowing time to review and refine job descriptions in light of changing needs, review progress toward ministry goals, identify areas for growth, establish new personal and ministry goals.
- Setting clear, specific objectives for each ministry area of responsibility.
- Encouraging self-assessment in light of established objectives.
- Having a staff development budget that associate staff members can use for personal and ministry development.

Practices that hinder:

- Not having clear ministry objectives for staff members' ministry areas.
- Avoiding performance reviews unless there is a significant problem.
- Not budgeting funds for staff and ministry development.
- Making performance reviews a "one-way" process by the supervisor, without drawing the staff member into the review process.

TAKING INVENTORY

We've covered a lot of issues above, and it can feel overwhelming to consider them all. We recommend taking some time to review these ten areas on your own and with your associate staff members and together determine which of the ten areas are "strengths," which are "adequate for now," and which are "areas for development." Then, select and tackle one of the "areas for development" at a time and see if you can find one or two things to work on that will help you make progress in that area. Be sure to take time to affirm the areas of "strengths" and those that are "adequate for now," and express appreciation to those who make these good things happen.

To help you in this reflection and assessment process, we've put together some questions that you as the team leader can consider, and some that would be good to discuss with your team members, either one-on-one, or all together. Focus your reflection and discussion on those that may be most helpful for you at this time.

Maintaining Clear Goals and Fostering Unified Commitment

Leader: Do I see any evidence of "ministry drift" in any of our ministry areas? How long has it been since I led our team in reviewing and clarifying our ministry purposes and goals? When might it be good to revisit this?

Together or One-on-One: Are we all clear on our church's purposes and ministry goals? Do we each understand how our ministry areas fit with and help accomplish these purposes and goals? What significant progress is worth celebrating together and praising God for?

Clarifying Roles, Responsibilities, Procedures, and Processes

Leader: Do I see any evidence of confusion by staff members regarding their roles and responsibilities or their understanding of procedures and processes here at the church? Do we have updated job descriptions that address these areas? Have our staff members received adequate orientation on how we do things here?

Together or One-on-One: Are we all clear on our roles and responsibilities on staff? Have there been any recent changes that have made this a bit unclear? Has anyone had challenges in understanding how to get certain things approved or done? What needs clarification?

Keeping Communication Open and Clear

Leader: Do I sense that there is open communication with and among our staff? Am I being a good example in my own communication with my team members? Have I allowed conflicts to simmer, making communication and collaboration more difficult?

Together or One-on-One: Are we setting aside enough time, often enough, to communicate well together? What good examples of clear and open communication have you observed recently that should be affirmed? Where do you think we need some additional effort?

Developing a Collaborative Climate

Leader: Do you observe team members collaborating well, or do they seem to be working in their own "silos" or actively competing with one another for scarce resources? When there has been a need for different departments or ministry areas to collaborate, has it seemed to go well, or were there challenges? What seemed to be the problem(s)?

Together or One-on-One: Do you ever feel as though you are having to compete with other ministry areas for resources or support? When you have wanted to pursue a ministry initiative that involved working with a colleague, have you felt that it went well, or was it hard to do? If it was a challenge, what made it difficult?

Drawing on Each Other's Strengths

Leader: Do you publicly affirm the gifts and strengths of your team members? Do you allow them to take a significant role in a ministry effort that you are also involved in? As you consider your work relationship with your team, are you feeling any jealousies or insecurities that make it hard to work together as you should? If so, are you seeking God's help to overcome these?

Together or One-on-One: Do you feel that your gifts and strengths in ministry are being developed and affirmed? Are there areas of ministry need in the church where you think you may have something to contribute, but there has not been the opportunity to assist? How can we guard against pride and jealousy as we work together for God's purposes?

Setting and Communicating Priorities

Leader: Do I lead our team in regularly reviewing our ministry priorities as a church? Am I helping team members sort through the many demands they face and set priorities for their ministry areas? Have I taken time recently to celebrate and affirm significant accomplishments and good progress in ministry by the team?

Together or One-on-One: Do any of us feel confused or overwhelmed with the number of ministry tasks we are supposed to be accomplishing? Do we feel like the work pressure never ends, and there is no real sense of accomplishment? What might we do together to recognize significant accomplishments that God has brought about in our ministries?

Establishing Standards of Excellence

Leader: Am I modeling the kinds of standards of excellence in ministry that I desire from members of our ministry team? Have I taken time to discuss these with the team to ensure we are in agreement and pursuing these standards together? Do I take time to affirm team members for meeting these kinds of standards?

Together or One-on-One: Do we have a good sense of the ministry standards we are aiming for? Do we feel comfortable talking about this together, and raising concerns if we think we are not achieving these well? Do we feel affirmed when we work hard to reach these standards?

Building Team Morale over Time

Leader: What indicators do I see that our team morale is healthy or not? Is there anyone who seems discouraged or stressed who could benefit from my encouragement? What do I communicate to others by my own spirit in the midst of our ministry challenges? How can I help team members focus on God's grace and provision, and the positive outcomes I see?

Together or One-on-One: If we are able to be honest with each other, what is encouraging us, and what is discouraging us in our ministry settings? Are any of us feeling overwhelmed? What kind of support and encouragement are we needing at this time?

Fostering External Support—in the Church and from God

Leader: Do I lead our team in regularly seeking God's guidance and aid in our ministry efforts? Do I advocate for our team members and their ministry areas with our church boards and congregational leaders? Am I keeping our congregation aware of what is happening in the various ministries of the church, and the kinds of support needed to maintain their effectiveness?

Together or One-on-One: Are we together adequately seeking God's guidance and aid in our ministries, or do we seem to have a spirit of self-sufficiency? Do we feel that the congregation is aware of our ministry area successes and needs? As your ministry responsibilities have grown, have you felt that the resources and support have kept up with your work demands?

Assessing and Developing Team Members

Leader: Do you have regular times for debriefing and assessment with each of the team members? Have you worked with each of them to set clear and specific objectives for the coming months or year? Do you have a budget, and clear processes for using it, for staff development?

Together or One-on-One: Do you feel that you are getting adequate, timely discussion and feedback on how things are going in your ministry areas? Do you feel clear on what the objectives and goals are that you should be pursuing in your ministry areas? Are there areas where you feel you need to learn and grow in order to handle your responsibilities well? If so, what resources or learning opportunities do you think would be most helpful?

Following Up: In light of what I have considered and/or we have discussed above, what needs to be given priority and addressed in the near future? What is important but can wait a while before we address it? When and where will these items be followed up on?

Chapter Three

Time Together, Part I

Constructive Regular Team Meetings

Kevin E. Lawson

A TALE OF TWO TEAM MEETINGS

"It was the worst of times, it was the best of times."[1] I'm talking about the contrast between two different experiences of church staff meetings during my years as an associate staff member. In both cases, we had regular weekly meetings together as pastoral staff, but they were so radically different experiences that each had a deep impact on me.

The Worst of Times: In one setting we met weekly at a restaurant for breakfast, reviewed recent ministry efforts, and discussed all of the needs and challenges that we were facing. Then we left. While these times kept me informed of what we needed to address, there was little time spent in identifying good progress, giving thanks for God's grace and provision, or personal sharing. In two years together, we never prayed together as a staff, not at these meetings, or in any other setting. Over time, I found that I left these meetings with a heavy heart, burdened by the constant review of the needs and challenges we faced. Twice, when I asked about taking time to pray together, it was met with agreement, but it never happened, and I was too young and new to push for it. It was discouraging to my soul.

The Best of Times: Years later, in a different church, we met weekly in the pastor's office. Time was spent reading Scripture, sharing about both personal and ministry issues, reviewing recent ministry efforts and progress, and discussing the needs and challenges we faced. We took time to plan and troubleshoot together and to pray for one another, the needs of members of our church, and our ministry together. I found a sense of fellowship and support within the group. We each had our own ministry areas, but we cared about and supported one another, and at times we collaborated on different ministry efforts. I found that I looked forward to these gatherings, sharing intimately, assessing and planning, and praying together. The work was just as heavy, but I was encouraged in my soul as we tackled it together.

THE IMPORTANCE OF TIME TOGETHER
AND USING IT WELL

In the last chapter, we looked at several priorities and practices for teamwork together with associate staff members. In looking them over, there is one thing that stands out clearly: for the majority of the items we presented, clear and accurate communication in a supportive environment is foundational to achieving them well. Whether it is

- maintaining goals and fostering unified commitment together;
- clarifying roles, responsibilities, procedures, and processes;
- developing a collaborative climate;
- setting and communicating priorities;
- establishing standards of excellence;
- building team morale; or
- assessing and developing team members,

none of these are possible without good communication together among the ministry staff.

While much can be accomplished in written documents, e-mails, and texts, it is in time spent together that the richest, fullest communication is possible. Supervising pastors who want to see their associate staff work well together as a team invest heavily in face-to-face communication. It is the "oil in the machinery" that reduces friction and allows us to coordinate our efforts well. Without it, things heat up, parts seize up, and before you know it, things have broken down (just like the car one of my children let run out of oil many years ago).

As we spoke with pastors whose associates felt were exemplary in their supervision practices, they emphasized over and over again how important their times together talking in meetings were for working well as a team. For some, setting aside this kind of time together came naturally; for others it did not, but it was a priority they established and a valuable discipline they developed over time. One pastor talked about his own negative experience as an associate staff member and how it helped him make regular meetings with his associate staff a priority.

The previous place I was at, the lead pastor cancelled them [staff meetings] at least half the time, last minute. Just never felt important. . . . Here we meet very regularly, every Wednesday, 10 o'clock. It's a chance where Pastor [name] can share . . . keep things coming up, what we're trying to accomplish at the church, how do the different people's roles fit together . . . if there's any area where we need the youth or the kid's ministry, or the music ministry, creative arts ministry, how they can support what we're doing, any admin stuff. But it's also a chance they can tell us about things they're doing in their own ministries, things they're trying to accomplish. Helps a little bit breaking that silo mentality, like "Hey I do my thing you do yours, and we're only going to talk if we have problems."

For this pastor, regular meeting time together helped reduce the sense of isolation, independent ministry focus, and lack of communication that comes with a "ministry silo" mentality. Another supervisor expressed how the time they spend together in their regular meetings helps build their sense of mutual support and being a ministry team.

. . . we have that time kind of built in where we all know we're going to be here, and we basically have to have permission to miss that meeting. So it kind of keeps that continuity. I think it's really important because I've been in places like I said, my last church, where you're just kind of out there doing your own thing. Hey you get your stuff done and I'll get my stuff done and hopefully you won't bother me. You don't really feel like you have a lot of support or that you're part of a team when it's like that.

We also heard another supervisor reflect on how informal one-on-one meetings with staff members are not necessarily always something he feels he needs, but it allowed an opportunity to give feedback and to reassure the associate staff of the value of their work and to build them up.

We have a lot of people that work hard and try to grow and do their best, and we're very committed. Sometimes that makes you feel like you don't need regular meetings. . . . But at the same time I know they need feedback to know they're doing a good job. It's not like there's a lot of problems to correct or address, so . . . in those informal meetings I really try to say, "Hey I see this, or heard that," try to give them compliments. . . .

Meetings, face-to-face, in groups, or one-on-one, are the major way we communicate with each other and facilitate the critical aspects of working well together. When these meetings are done well, there is a strong sense of unity, mutual support, and cooperation; clear understanding of roles and responsibilities; and a spirit of hope. When these meetings are neglected or are not done well, they can undermine the ability of church staff to work well together, creating a sense of isolation, insecurity, conflict, or competition, and a loss of direction and purpose. Learning how to use your time together well as you meet may be your biggest investment in fostering a strong ministry team.

THREE KINDS OF MEETINGS

In any church setting where there are three or more staff members, there tend
to be three different kinds of meetings of staff that are beneficial to their
work together. The first kind of meeting is the *Regular Team Meeting*, held
every week or two where there is time for reviewing recent ministry activities and needs and planning for upcoming efforts. The second kind of meeting is the *Occasional Team Gathering*, held less often, some perhaps only
annually, where extended time is given for focused attention on other kinds
of major concerns, like long-range planning, training, or personal spiritual
formation. Finally, the third kind of meeting is the *One-on-One*, where the
supervisor meets with the individual staff member for more focused discussion and personal interaction than is possible in the regular team meeting. On
church staffs where there are only two people, the regular team meeting is a
one-on-one, facilitating the goals of each simultaneously.

In this chapter, we'll be taking a close look at the first kind of group
meeting, the *Regular Team Meeting*, and how to make them constructive and
beneficial for you and your associate staff members. In the next chapter we'll
take a closer look at *Occasional Team Gatherings* and *One-on-One* meetings
and what can make these invaluable for your work together. As we examine
these different kinds of meetings, we'll hear from both supervisors and
associate staff members as they share from their experience about what
makes these meetings most profitable, strengthening their work together.

Planning Your *Regular Team Meetings*

Regular Team Meetings are the lifeblood of a ministry team. Because they
are regular, on everyone's calendar, team members know that there is time
set aside soon to talk through issues or questions that have arisen over the last
week or so. They know the rhythm of these meetings, the scope of what will
be addressed, and what they can expect from this time together. This allows
everyone to determine which issues can wait until that meeting and what
needs to be addressed outside of that group gathering. Every supervising
pastor we interviewed talked about the importance and value of these meetings, and shared with us their approaches to them. The associate staff members who participated in our survey described the benefit of these regular
meetings for themselves and their ministry. In reviewing what they all
shared, we found there were five common elements of these meetings that
seemed to be key to making them most beneficial for everyone involved.
We'll describe these five elements below, but first let's consider a few
basic issues regarding the scheduling of these *Regular Team Meetings*.

How Often? The most common approach we heard from supervising
pastors about how often they met with their associate staff as a group was

"once a week." This allowed a careful, timely review of the ministry efforts of the previous week, with special focus on the worship and educational ministry efforts of the last weekend. Some supervising pastors only do this kind of group meeting once every two weeks, but that was much less common.

When? There was a bit of variation on when these *Regular Team Meetings* were held. Most supervisors tried to find a time shortly after weekend ministry efforts to hold this meeting, such as Monday or Tuesday, but others waited until Wednesday to meet. This tended to revolve around when pastoral staff took their days off and when everyone was available to meet. Aiming for early in the week allowed time for review of the weekend's ministry while it was still fairly fresh in everyone's mind, and also ensured there was enough time to prepare well for the coming weekend. This weekly rhythm of ministry shaped the frequency and timing of these regular meetings.

Where? Typically, these meetings were held on the church campus. In some cases, if the senior pastor's office was large enough, the group met there. The main issue was to find a quiet, comfortable space where they could give focused attention to each other, uninterrupted. The privacy of meeting on the church campus seemed to fit well for these group gatherings.

For How Long? This depends a lot on the scope of the agenda and the size of the group. Some supervising pastors we spoke with talked about meetings that lasted as short as an hour and a quarter. Others had meetings going over three hours, with a meal included. The purposes of the meeting and size of the group will dictate how long it will take to accomplish what is needed. As you work through this chapter and consider what you want to do with your *Regular Team Meetings*, consider realistically how much time will be needed to work through the agenda without being rushed. In some cases, you may opt to include some agenda items weekly, and other items rotating in and out over a period of several weeks.

Who Is Present? In most cases, these meetings included all full-time pastoral staff members. In some cases, these included part-time pastoral staff as well, and some even had one or more of the church board members, who attended when available. You will need to think through whom you want present at these regular meetings, and who might be invited on occasion to participate. There may even be people whom you invite for a part of the meeting, but then have them leave if other portions of the meeting are not relevant for them. Some larger churches bring in their part-time ministry directors on occasion for part of a meeting to hear from them and pray for their personal needs and ministry efforts.

What To Focus On? As we listened to the supervising pastors we interviewed, they described a variety of things that they did in their *Regular Team Meetings* with their associate staff members, with five of these things being especially important. While not every leader did all five of them in every meeting, most were done every week, and others were high priorities that made it onto the agenda on a rotating basis. Let's look together at these five elements (table 3.1), why they are important, and what helps the group do them well. We've framed the five elements as "looking" in different directions.

LOOKING UP: Attending to God through Scripture, Prayer, Worship. While the ways that this was carried out varied from one supervising pastor to another, each made sure that there was time set aside in their *Regular Team Meetings* for personal sharing and prayer together for each other and the ministries they were involved in. In many cases, time was also set aside for studying the Scripture or taking turns sharing devotionals together to unite their focus on God, who had called and equipped them for ministry together. While it was not always first on the agenda, it was a high priority that was seen as crucial for the team as they met together. One pastor shares their team's practices and why he feels this investment is so important.

> *Every Wednesday from ten to noon, we have our weekly staff meeting. How that staff meeting's structured is the first half hour is given to some type of devotional and prayer time together. So it's almost like a cell-group, family group, life group. And the reason for that is, I feel like our staff members are always pouring out to others, it's kind of a time where I feel like I need to pour into them. So we do devotions together, and then we pray for one another, and that's the first thing on the agenda. I don't lead all of that, I do the majority, but sometimes we divide that up, and we'll have a different staff member share how God's working in their life or growing them.*

Another supervisor describes their practices and some of the spontaneity of prayer that they have together. Given the challenges that they face together in ministry, prayer together is a natural response, both in large group gatherings and individually.

Table 3.1.   Five Key Elements of *Regular Team Meetings*

Looking Up:	Attending to God through Scripture, Prayer, Worship
Looking Back:	Reviewing Recent Ministry Efforts, Renewing Vision
Looking Ahead:	Planning and Preparing for Future Ministry Efforts
Looking Inside:	Promoting Fellowship, Unity, Mutual Support
Looking Outside:	Learning and Growing Together in Meetings

Well, we always have a time of prayer at our weekly staff meetings. We open with some sort of devotion or training, there's usually some spiritual element to that, but we always open with prayer. Usually we stop a couple times during the staff meeting to pray for some things specific to the church, or if somebody's facing some real challenges on the staff. Sometimes we'll pair up and we'll pray for each other, sometimes share prayer requests. Not every week, you know with 12 people that could take quite a bit of time. Comes out in different ways, I pray with people frequently when I meet with them, pray with them about stuff going on.

Several of the supervising pastors ensure that there is significant time spent attending to the personal prayer needs of the team members, together lifting up the needs of those who are serving the needs of others in the church. One describes what this looks like at their staff meetings.

We have a staff meeting every Monday, that basically goes from 11 to 2:30, and when we meet at 11 o'clock it's for pastoral staff and families, prayer support. And we literally just come into our conference room, sit down and say, how are you guys doing, and who can we pray for? It becomes a very transparent, active, honest time of saying things like "hey I'm looking for a new car" or "my mom's being admitted to a care home for dementia" or "I got a doctor's appointment" or "I've got a real difficult person in my ministry." And we spend anywhere from 30–45 minutes every Monday praying for each other when someone says "Hey I've got a prayer request," and someone else will volunteer and we'll stop right there and pray for them, and say amen, and whoever's next says "I could use prayer for . . . ." We literally walk through that one prayer request at a time until we're done, and that's one thing we do, and it happens every Monday.

Another supervisor describes how the team spends time praying for the needs of others in the church, and for the different ministries, and makes sure they take time to revisit past needs they have prayed about so that they can give thanks to God for answered prayer. They want to make sure they acknowledge God's goodness and provision, not just ask about new needs all of the time.

And we eat lunch together from 11:45–12:15–30, and then we pray together for all the requests that come in, and then we spend, the next one's a crucial one, we spend time doing what we call praises. For the longest time I noted it, it suddenly dawned on me, we're praying for all the staff requests, we're praying for all the church requests, but we're never taking time to acknowledge answers. So we cover that under praises, answers for our kids, answers for our ministry, who came to Christ, how well the meeting went. And it serves two purposes, it allows us to celebrate, but it also allows everyone an opportunity to know what's going on, and what's going on well in other people's ministries.

Finally, one of the supervising pastors we talked with reflected on his experience as an associate staff member joining a church staff team where prayer together was *not* part of their practice. In some ways it seemed symptomatic of their lack of being a team together in ministry. It requires openness, support, and caring for one another, and a measure of intimacy for meaningful prayer together.

> *We all sat down, everybody opened their Day-Timer, and they all jumped into the calendar, and I was pretty naive at that time, and I just raised my hand and said, "Hey guys don't you think it would be a good idea if we prayed first, really ask God to guide us? Can we have a prayer?" And the pastor gave me a very dirty look, he said a very quick prayer, and that was the first and last time we ever prayed together as a staff, for two years. And it was just, I loved my job, I loved working with my students, and God blessed it and grew it, but man there was no team, there was no unity, there was no "we're in this together" and I felt very isolated and on my own. Yeah, it was horrible.*

Given the spiritual battles that can come with ministry leadership, and the great needs we see around us in our congregations and ministries, time together listening to God through Scripture, and praying together, is foundational to a strong ministry team. Making this a priority in your *Regular Team Meetings* is a key part of uniting in ministry.

LOOKING BACK: Reviewing Recent Ministry Efforts, Renewing Vision. Every supervisor we listened to described how an important part of their *Regular Team Meetings* was reviewing recent ministry efforts. Many times they just mentioned it without elaboration, assuming that this was something commonly understood as important. In their team meetings, time was set aside to reflect on what was going well, where there were challenges, and where things needed to be done differently. Because of the weekly rhythm of worship and ministry programs with children, youth, and adults, a lot of the "looking back" time is focused on these weekly activities, along with any special events that have taken place since the last team meeting. One pastor describes how their team approaches this aspect of their meeting time.

> *But one of my primary responsibilities is over the weekend services, and we do a weekly evaluation meeting where we go through and break down the service. We talk about what we need to sharpen, what we need to fix, we do weekly planning meetings. People are held accountable to their assignments. I think most people on our staff would probably say that I'm a little too nice, but at the same time there's a high degree of accountability.*

Taking time for "looking back" allows supervisors to accomplish several things that are beneficial for members of the ministry team. These include:

Reviewing: What has been going on in the different ministry areas of the church? Don't assume that everyone is aware of what is happening in each ministry department. It's also helpful, before looking ahead at what is coming up soon, to be reminded of what we have been working on and what has been accomplished.

Assessing: It is amazing how often, in the light of the pressing needs in front of us, we fail to adequately debrief and learn from our recent ministry efforts. But there is wisdom in taking time to reflect on what went well, what we can learn and do better next time, which ministry efforts are showing fruitfulness, and which ones may need some retooling. An environment that invites honest assessment without defensiveness is needed, one where the desire to do better is stronger than the desire to be praised.

Troubleshooting: One of the results of careful assessment is recognizing where there are challenges or problems that need to be addressed, allowing the team to discuss them together and find solutions. Taking time to look back allows this kind of learning and improvement to take place.

Celebrating: Sometimes, as we assess recent ministry efforts, the appropriate response is one of praise to God and joyful celebration. Assessment need not always be critical, and we would indeed be ungrateful if we did not take time to recognize God's goodness in the midst of our ministry. We have to be careful that we don't subtly communicate a sense that nothing is ever good enough. One associate pastor, reflecting on her supervisor's tendencies, shares this caution.

> *I think sometimes, one of our questions on our weekly thing is, "Hey what do we do good?" But it's always, what could we have done better? So it's good to see that, but, it's also, let's celebrate what we just did well together. But I think [pastor], because he's a bit more of a perfectionist, is like, "Okay, how can we tweak it just a little bit better?"*

Renewing Vision: Sometimes, under the pressures and demands of ministry, our sense of purpose and ministry vision can get blurred and dulled. Part of "looking back" is to remind ourselves of what we are called to do as a church, how our ministry areas and personal ministry roles are helping the church fulfill its calling, and what goals we are striving to achieve in the near future. Don't assume (as I have at times) that everyone has a strong sense of our common purpose and a clear sense of the value of their ministry efforts. We need times of vision renewal, and this can be done in *Regular Team Meetings* through reminders by the team leader of our purpose, calling, and goals. Investing a few minutes in revisiting these important foundations helps maintain a team's sense of purpose and unity.

LOOKING AHEAD: Planning and Preparing for Future Ministry Efforts. Not surprisingly, another major part of *Regular Team Meetings* is planning for future ministry efforts. This is critical for coordinating efforts together, supporting one another, and ensuring buy-in from all involved when new things are being proposed. Expectations, roles, and responsibilities can be confirmed and clarified, needs expressed, resources allocated, and coordination of effort ensured.

After describing the time invested in the early part of their team meetings in spiritual focus and prayer, this pastor explains how they use the latter half of their meeting time to prepare for the ministry ahead of them:

> *. . . then the last hour is really devoted to doing the work. What's coming up, what's on the calendar, what are our plans, what needs to be communicated. So there's kind of like, there's a 50/50, the first half of the meeting is soul care, family development, the other 50% is the business. Family business. Family first, and then business. So that's how we structure our staff meeting.*

Sometimes, as new ministry initiatives are being proposed or presented by different team members, it is good to allow enough time for others impacted by these initiatives to ask questions and offer their perspectives on what might be important to consider. This can help unify the group behind the ministry effort, and possibly shape it in light of the wisdom of the group. Team leaders can benefit from taking time for this kind of discussion, as shared by one supervising pastor.

> *That's a concrete practice for me that I say to myself: make sure I listen to this person, make sure this person feels heard; . . . if you want to get the buy-in of a person that you're supervising, they have to feel heard. Then they're willing to let go, . . . "we have to do things my way," that sort of thing, or . . . I want to do this this way. Then they're able to hear other suggestions.*

Part of looking ahead is making decisions, and then ensuring that there is clarity regarding who is responsible to follow through and who needs to be informed of the decisions so that things can move forward smoothly. One supervising pastor shares some of the frustrations that come when things are not clear and how important it is to nail down clarity, not just be content with general decisions.

> *I think another big thing for me was just being really clear on what decisions we had made, and what the expectations were in terms of execution. I've been in so many meetings with staff and teams, where we come out and it's not really clear, what was the decision we just made? Who needs to know the decision we just made? And who is responsible for what? And getting clarity around those things really gives people traction of where they need to spend their time and focus.*

It can be helpful to take time before the meeting ends to review quickly what was decided, who is now following up, and any particular things that need to be done next.

Finally, to make "looking ahead" a productive part of your meeting together, it can help to send out an agenda ahead of time with some of the basic information included about the future ministry efforts you will be discussing, especially any decisions that will need to be made, and any information you want team members to bring to the meeting, or any questions you want them to come prepared to discuss. This provides time for prayerful reflection and careful consideration, helping make best use of the limited time you have together at the meeting.

LOOKING INSIDE: Promoting Fellowship, Unity, Mutual Support. *Regular Team Meetings* are also an opportunity to promote a growing sense of connection, of fellowship together in the midst of ministry challenges and opportunities. Taking time for personal sharing and prayer, as described above, is one major way of building this sense of fellowship, but there is more that can be done to grow in supporting one another.

Regular Team Meetings are opportunities to give attention to encouraging and building each other up. In 1 Thessalonians 5:11, after Paul had reflected on the return of Christ and our salvation in Christ, he said, "Therefore encourage one another and build one another up, just as you are doing." Also, in Galatians 6:9, he says, "And let us not grow weary of doing good, for in due season we will reap, if we do not give up." *Regular Team Meetings* provide a time for encouraging each other and helping each other not grow weary in the midst of the ministries God has called you to. Given the discouragements, and the weariness that can come from heavy ministry demands and challenges, encouraging one another at team meetings is an important ministry to one another. Some of us need this more than others. One pastor, reflecting on the personality differences seen among their team members, commented:

> *People aren't like me. That one is very big; a huge lesson that I try to remind myself that when I talk with [name] and I talk with [name], they're not me. They think differently and they value different things. I don't need a lot of warm fuzzies, or a high-touch kind of thing, but some people do, so I think that's a huge turning point for me.*

We are different from each other, and ministry team leaders are aware of this and provide what team members need in encouragement. Encouragement can come from all members of the team, not just the team leader. Encouraging and affirming one another is a great way to build the fellowship and mutual support of the team. Another supervisor describes how this is done in their church team meetings.

And even the way we do our staff meetings, we try to keep that fun and relational. We always start off with, "hey what are some ministry wins," but some weeks we'll switch it and now you have to point out something great that you saw in another ministry. Publicly encouraging each other builds that as well.

In the midst of accomplishing the work of ministry together as a team, wise supervisors take time to build a strong fellowship among team members, and encourage a ministry of mutual encouragement in the midst of the personal and work challenges group members face.

LOOKING OUTSIDE: Learning and Growing Together in Meetings. Finally, one of the five key elements of *Regular Team Meetings* that is beneficial, but may not be included every time you meet, is taking time to learn and grow together by reading and discussing articles, blogs, podcasts, and books relevant for team members' personal or ministry development. The supervisors we listened to shared how this was an important aspect of their *Regular Team Meetings*, providing time to learn and grow together, providing stimulus to their thinking and their personal development as leaders. One pastor describes their team's perspective and practices this way:

. . . there's a section of the staff meeting that's designated to promote growth or development. Sometimes we will read a book together, and we'll talk about the book that we're all reading as a staff, and we've read several books together as a staff, just to keep us growing and sharpening. We have this mantra where we go, "Growing people grow people." And so if we stop growing, we're not going to grow anybody under our ministry. Kind of dependent on our focus. We'll pick a book that's going to help us develop, everything from John Maxwell's Twenty-one Irrefutable Laws of Leadership, *we read that book together.*

Another pastor shares their basic approach.

Once a month we'll sit down and typically we'll go through a book together. We kind of fluctuate between a leadership book or a theology book, something like that.

An associate staff member describes how their team leader devoted time in meetings to discussing books they were reading, one chapter a week.

We just finished reading a book together on the life of Joshua, Called to be God's Leader, *by Henry Blackaby. It was lessons from the life of Joshua, and it was about spiritual leadership. We each read a chapter each week and then discuss it together. Sometimes he'll bring something from his devotional time, or we've read through leadership books like* Courageous Leadership, *by Bill Hybels, or something like that. We've read articles that people have brought to his attention or he came across, and we'll discuss how we apply that as a church, as a team.*

Another way of learning and growing together is when different team members attend conferences and then take time to debrief the whole team on what they learned that they think would be beneficial for the church. One supervisor gives an example of how this works out in their church.

> *Our children's ministry leader, she goes to a children's pastors conference, we don't go to that one with her, but we ask her when she comes back to share some of the things that she got out of it and that maybe the church needs to be aware of.*

Finally, depending on the resources around you, it may be possible to invite a guest with extensive ministry experience in an area of need you are facing at your church to join your team meeting so you can interact and learn from her or him. Having a session and a meal together can help your team members think in new ways and be challenged and encouraged by someone who has faced the same kinds of ministry needs in another setting.

It can be easy to repeatedly postpone this kind of time investment, but the exemplary pastoral supervisors made it a priority to invest time in at least some of their *Regular Team Meetings* to identify and discuss insights they were learning from others that may strengthen and grow their team members and their ministries together. As the pastor said above, "Growing people grow people."

TAKING INVENTORY

We've reviewed the benefits of *Regular Team Meetings* and discussed five key aspects for making them constructive for you and your associate staff members. The benefits of these kinds of regular meetings may not always be immediately obvious to us as supervisors, but the problems that occur when these meetings are neglected, or do not address the five key aspects well, become evident over time. Attending to this well on a regular basis is one of the most important investments you can make to help your team work and thrive together in ministry for the long haul.

So, do you currently have regular meetings together with your associate staff? Are they as productive as you would like them to be? As in the last chapter, we've put together some questions that you as the team leader can consider and some that may be good to discuss with your team members. You may already have a sense of some areas that could be strengthened, so focus your reflection and discussion there. Take some time to consider these well and see if there might be ways to make your regular meetings even more beneficial for you and your associate staff members.

Logistical Aspects of RTMs

Leader: Is our pattern of RTMs adequate for all that we want and need to accomplish together? Are there people we should include, at least on occasion, whom we need to hear from and also support in their work?

Together: Is our schedule for our RTMs a good one for you, or does it create challenges due to other commitments or responsibilities? If we had more time available in our RTMs, what would you like to see us do together that we've not had adequate time for in the past?

Looking Up

Leader: To what degree is this a regular part of your time together? Do you feel limited in this area due to time demands? What are some ways this aspect of your meetings could be strengthened and take a higher priority? Do you feel comfortable involving other team members in helping to lead this?

Together: What do you appreciate about the times of sharing and prayer we've had in the group? What would you value doing if this were to be expanded in any way? Would you feel comfortable helping lead this aspect of our time together?

Looking Back

Leader: Is your agenda so crowded with upcoming needs and events that you don't take much time for debriefing recent ministry efforts? How are you occasionally revisiting and reinforcing your church's mission and vision for ministry with your team? How can you debrief recent ministry efforts in ways that help your team learn and plan better for the future?

Together: What do you think would help us debrief recent ministry efforts well in our RTMs? Are there times when our sense of mission and purpose for your ministry seems confused or clouded over? What could we do together in our meetings to renew our sense of purpose together?

Looking Ahead

Leader: When it comes to planning and preparing for future ministry efforts, is your team getting enough time to discuss implications of ministry decisions? Do they seem clear on their responsibilities and how to proceed once the meeting is over? What kind of follow-up on your part would help ensure clarity? Would an agenda before the meeting help people prepare for our conversations and make better use of our time for discussion?

Together: Do you feel that we generally take enough time discussing ministry decisions and plans for upcoming activities? If not, what would be helpful to ensure that we do at each meeting? As decisions are made and the meeting ends, do you sometimes feel confused about your responsibilities and how to proceed?

Looking Inside

Leader: When you meet with your team, are you taking time for encouraging feedback? Do you have a sense that the group members feel connected with and supportive of one another, or do they seem to lack a sense of fellowship in their work together? What might you do in your meeting times to try to grow a stronger sense of mutual support and encouragement?

Together: When we meet, do you feel encouraged and supported in your ministry, or have we not given enough attention to this as part of our ministry with one another? What do you think would help us build a stronger sense of mutual encouragement and support?

Looking Outside

Leader: In your RTMs, do you occasionally take time for discussing materials by ministry leaders that you think would be beneficial for the personal growth of the team or the development of your ministries? What have you found to be most beneficial for your team? If time feels too limited for doing this on a regular basis, how often could you create special times for this kind of investment in learning together?

Together: If your RTMs have included time for discussing ministry leadership materials, what have you found most beneficial in those times? What would you like to see the group do together if time allowed?

Following Up: In light of what I have considered and/or we have discussed above, what needs to be given priority and addressed in the near future? What is important, but can wait a while before we address it? When and where will these items be followed up on?

Chapter Four

Time Together, Part II

*Profitable Occasional Team
Gatherings and One-on-Ones*

Kevin E. Lawson

REMEMBERING TIME AWAY TOGETHER

For several years now, I've been serving as an overseer, or elder, on my church board. In the first few years as an overseer board, we had two "regular team"–type meetings a month, many of which would last four hours or more. We were expanding and establishing multi-site ministry campuses, multiplying pastoral staff and overseers, which made our decision processes more complicated. Many times, it seemed as though the regular agenda items took up so much time that there was little time and energy left for discussion of larger issues. Our regular meetings had such packed agendas that time for reflective conversation felt limited. We tried not to let these larger issues get squeezed out, which is why our meetings tended to go on so long. One of the things that helped us in this challenging time was our annual Overseers' Retreat. We would spend two nights and parts of three days together at a rented lodge and slow our pace down to more carefully examine critical, foundational, ministry issues, helping set our direction and agenda for the coming year. We also cooked together, ate together, and had time for coffee and conversation there and as we carpooled to and from the retreat. These retreats have been invaluable for building relationships and helping us work through major issues together that we just could not accomplish in the confines of our "regular" meetings. I've now had to step off the board for a time, and I miss these retreats with our pastors and overseers.

Our last chapter focused on the importance of *Regular Team Meetings* and valuable aspects to build into these times together with all of the associate staff. In this chapter, we're going to consider two other kinds of meetings and how to carry them out in ways that promote working well as a ministry team and thriving together as you do so. The first is four different kinds of *Occasional Team Gatherings* that can supplement what you accomplish in your regular meetings, and the second is how to make your *One-on-One* meetings with your supervisees beneficial for them and for you. Let's begin with a look at *Occasional Team Gatherings*, like the annual retreat I described above.

BEYOND THE *REGULAR TEAM MEETINGS*: VALUABLE *OCCASIONAL TEAM GATHERINGS*

As I shared above, there is only so much you can do in your *Regular Team Meetings*. The weekly demands of pastoral work make it difficult to find time for tackling bigger, more complex issues, or for extended time in prayer or discussion together on foundational matters. The exemplary supervisors we interviewed shared with us about the different kinds of special gatherings that they had from time to time with their associate staff members. Some of their gatherings combined more than one of the purposes that we will describe below, but they can generally be categorized into one of the following four types of events (table 4.1).

SPIRITUAL RETREATS: Pursuing Spiritual Vitality, Deepening Relationships. One of the subtle traps that we know we have to be careful of in ministry leadership roles is that of relentlessly pouring out in serving the needs of others without taking adequate time for pursuing our own spiritual health and vitality. In addition, when a ministry team spends all of their time in ministry assessment and planning, it can put too much of a focus on our own efforts for God rather than on His efforts for and through us. One of the ways to promote a strong spiritual life among those on the ministry team is to intentionally set aside times for focused spiritual renewal together, ensuring

Table 4.1.   Four Common Types of *Occasional Team Gatherings*

Spiritual Retreats:	Pursuing Spiritual Vitality, Deepening Relationships
Planning Retreats:	Discernment, Long-Range Planning, Unity in Ministry
Conferences & Seminars:	Learning Together Away
Socials & Celebrations:	Fellowship Together as Staff, as Families

that this is a high value for our team and for each of us personally as we follow God's calling. In addition to making Scripture reading and prayer a part of *Regular Team Meetings*, the supervisors we talked with described how important occasional times away together in spiritual retreat were for their work together with associate staff. One pastor describes the value of their practice of quarterly prayer retreats:

> *I'm putting pretty high value on prayer ministry in the church, and one of the things I try to schedule quarterly is to take the staff away from the campus for, I call it a half-day of prayer. And I've tried to teach them and give them some formats for how to spend some time in personal worship, reflection, anticipation, cleansing, asking God. "Search me oh God, know my heart," kind of thing. That's a team event that we do off campus.*

Other supervising pastors held these kinds of retreats with their staff once a year. However often they were done, it was important to them to ensure that this was part of how they did ministry together, drawing near to God together and seeking God's grace and strength personally and for their ministries. In some cases, these were events that they organized on their own, but some took advantage of pastoral retreats being put on by different conference centers.

For some ministry team leaders, another part of these kinds of spiritual retreats has been the opportunity to promote deeper sharing and understanding of one another among the team members. The agendas and pace of weekly meetings may not allow time for this level of sharing, so retreats away together can be a great time for building deeper relationships. One pastor explains how they use their time on retreats for sharing that takes them deeper in knowing one another.

> *So a couple of things that I've done to try to address that very issue is to try to do a genogram with people on the team. So that people kind of understand their own spiritual journey, and some of the baggage that they may bring into their role. Another question I love to ask in a team environment is what is it from your past that would be helpful for people to know in working with you?*

Some supervising pastors have expanded this kind of retreat to include spouses as well. They see the importance of promoting healthy growth together between staff members and their spouses. It is not an easy thing to do, given work schedules and family demands, but it is something worth considering for the benefit of your associate staff members and their families.

> *I think retreats and getting away always works. It's really hard. . . . I think retreats with couples is super valuable, I'm not so sure it's not more valuable than just getting away with your own staff. But when you've got little children involved, that's a tough animal to pull off. . . . One of our greatest challenges*

is how do we pull the wives into this thing, because so much of it is the husband-wife relationship, which you all know, you get the overflow at church. Or church can become an escape from that, or all kinds of wrong stuff.

PLANNING RETREATS: Discernment, Long-Range Planning, Unity in Ministry. A second kind of valuable "retreat" away together is the planning retreat. In some cases, these are overnight events away from the church for the church staff, sometimes with other lay leadership involved. In other cases, these are one-day events, allowing extended time for thinking, talking, and praying together about a coming season of ministry and how best to approach it in light of God's direction and the needs of the congregation. There are many ways that this kind of event can be done. One supervising pastor describes how they take time for retreats together, and for occasional planning days as a staff.

We do annual retreats at Hume Lake; they have a pastor's conference that we go to every year. . . . We do at least once or twice a year an all-day getaway, to plan and prepare and think.

The agendas and pace of *Regular Team Meetings* do not always allow adequate time for more careful reflection and conversation about the future direction of the church's ministry, how to prepare well ahead for major ministry initiatives, and having enough conversation together to help everyone "own" their part of the overall ministry effort, fostering a strong unity as they lead their ministry areas. Team leaders need to discern how often these kinds of work days together are needed and plan ahead to ensure all team members can participate without feeling stressed that they are not attending to other critical needs (e.g., not the day before VBS starts or the youth group leaves for a mission trip). When these kinds of planning retreats are done well, they renew vision, give direction for ministry, build unity, and put down the "big rocks" of ministry that other "smaller rocks" will be built around.

CONFERENCES & SEMINARS: Learning Together Away. We talked in the last chapter about ways of pursuing learning and growth together when you gather for your *Regular Team Meetings*. Another way of investing in the growth of your ministry team, and building relationships together, is to attend a conference or seminar together and take time for a thorough debriefing. Traveling together provides lots of time for conversation on a wide range of things, both personal and ministry related. The time spent after the event in debriefing, talking through what you learned, how something might be beneficial for the church, and where to begin pursuing it builds a stronger collaborative spirit, and a common understanding of how the ministry might be pursued in more beneficial ways. One associate reflects on his supervisor's approach, both with conferences and reading books together, and its impact on the staff.

> *We've been to several leadership conferences together, things he felt like he needs to learn or I need to learn; we go together and he has staff read through different books from time to time that will grow our leadership or help us in our spiritual commitment or walk. Kind of sharpen us, so we learn, study, and discuss together as a staff, so that's been really good.*

While major conferences can be expensive and take a lot of time out of your busy schedules, there may also be less expensive one-day seminars in your area that you can take advantage of. If you belong to a ministerial association in your community, you may want to talk with them about organizing training events that all of your church staffs could benefit from. Learning together is a valuable investment and worth the occasional expense to make it possible.

SOCIALS & CELEBRATIONS: Fellowship Together as Staff, as Families. I will never forget the Christmas gatherings we had when I was on church staff in Maine. Each year, our senior pastor and his wife organized an evening of wonderful food, conversation, and games. All of the staff, office and pastoral, came with their spouses. This was one of the highlights of the year for us, for we had a strong supportive relationship, and it was just so much fun to be together rejoicing in anticipation of celebrating Christmas. Each summer, we would have a similar kind of gathering, enjoying a great barbeque meal and fun together. These were rich times of fellowship that were part of our bond together. I know it took extra work on the part of our pastor and his wife, but it paid off in promoting our unity in ministry.

One other category of *Occasional Team Gatherings* that all of our supervising pastors talked about was the time they spent "off duty" having fun and celebrating ministry and personal joys together. For some, this seemed to come naturally, as part of the way they looked at their lives together with their fellow pastors. Others spoke out of a sense of intentionality, recognizing the value and benefit of these time investments, and ensuring they were scheduled on a regular basis. For example, one pastor describes their monthly ritual together as a staff this way:

> *First Monday of the month, whoever's birthday is that month, they pick the restaurant we go out to, we go out to eat together.*

On a larger scale, some supervisors include spouses in pastoral retreats, focusing the event more on relationship building and mutual support, but ensuring there is time for fun together.

We try to keep the pastor's retreat at Hume Lake to be purely fun; spouses go with us, we go to most of the meetings. We goof off together. We play games together at night. Last night we're all there we gather together at the camp-fires outside the dining hall there and pray for each other and our spouses. So that one's primarily have fun, goof off, play disc golf and all that.

There are many opportunities for these kinds of informal gatherings for social interaction and celebrations. They are a worthy investment in building a spirit of mutual support in ministry and enjoying the fellowship that you have together in ministry. Consider the range of ideas below, and come up with some of your own:

• a special dessert and celebration following a significant ministry success
• birthday celebrations on campus or out for lunch
• Christmas and Easter gatherings at a home or restaurant
• game night at the church or at someone's home
• pizza potluck dinner and "talent night"
• mini-golf outing and burgers
• coffee break together with home-baked goodies
• family picnics in a park
• progressive dinner
• retreats with spouses
• family beach day (or lake day) with barbeque
• concert night out, followed by dessert at a home (or preceded by dinner together)
• attending a "ball game" together (you pick the sport)
• baby shower for an expected child
• caroling together during Advent (and making Christmas cookies to share)

This is just to get you started. Find out what your team members, and their families, like to do, and make room in your schedules for some fun and fellowship together.

BEYOND THE REGULAR TEAM MEETINGS: PROFITABLE ONE-ON-ONE TIMES WITH ASSOCIATE STAFF

As important as *Regular Team Meetings* are, they will not, and cannot, take the place of having one-on-one times in conversation with each associate staff member you oversee. Whether these are scheduled on a regular basis, or happen frequently in an informal way, *One-on-Ones* are a critical part of supervision and support of your team members. Listen to a few of the associate staff members as they reflect on how their *One-on-Ones* with their supervisors are or were helpful to them.

My best supervising pastors met weekly with me, willing to discuss and pro-cess the aspects of my ministry area, plus bring me into their thoughts and ideas, which helped me get a better sense how they worked so I could work under them better.

My supervising pastor (a youth pastor) consistently met with me about both the ministry that I was leading and my personal life. We spent time discussing vision and planning together. I was given freedom to work on my own, but my supervising pastor spent time helping me to debrief different ministry events.

He made space for me within his own schedule. We met regularly to talk about ministry activities and personal growth. His presence was warm, understand-ing, & accepting. He drew from his own experiences, both positive & negative, in providing counsel and support. This helped me to overcome my own chal-lenges with less fear, knowing that those who've gone before me also dealt with similar obstacles in their paths.

One-on-Ones allow focused time with each of your associate staff to more carefully listen to them, debrief ministry events, consider upcoming needs, provide encouragement and correction, troubleshoot challenges, and more. The same major categories that are beneficial for *Regular Team Meetings* are also helpful to keep in mind when having *One-on-Ones* with your staff, but there is now more personal accountability, support, and mentoring that can take place as needed. A lot will depend on the personal and job maturity of the staff member. What I mean is that there will be a lot more variability in what these meetings focus on and how they are carried out due to the charac-ter, personality, and ministry experience of the person being supervised. But having the meetings on a somewhat regular basis provides a healthy context for communication, clarification, direction as needed, and support.

How can you make the most of your *One-on-One* times with your asso-ciate staff? Let's consider a few issues and practices that may help as you strive to make these meetings productive for your associates and yourself as a supervisor. But first, let's consider how an old leadership theory may still be relevant for the task of supervision of associate staff members as they grow on the job.

"Situational Leadership" and Tailoring Your *One-on-One* Meetings to Your Supervisees. In the late 1960s, Paul Hersey and Ken Blanchard introduced the Life Cycle Theory of Leadership, which later became known as the "Situational Leadership Model."[1] Their theory had a few basic ideas that are still relevant for thinking about how you might develop and use your *One-on-One* times well with your associate staff. Here are three foundational principles from their work:

1. There is no single best leadership style that fits everyone you might work with.
2. Part of determining how to lead someone will depend on the type of job the person is being asked to carry out.
3. Another part of determining how to lead someone will depend on both the relevant experience of the person and his or her willingness to take on the responsibilities of the job ("maturity level").

In a very general way, what they proposed was that when a person is new to a task, unable or insecure in carrying it out independently, then leadership needs to be more directive, providing clear instructions on what to do, when, how, and so on. They labeled this approach "Telling." If a person lacks experience, but is very willing to learn and is enthusiastic, then leadership needs to still give direction, but now allows more interaction in the process of the work, listening and responding to questions, and giving more encouragement and support. They labeled this approach "Selling." If the person is experienced and able to do the task, but lacks confidence to do it independently, the leader is able to be less directive, sharing the decision-making process and providing strong personal encouragement and support. They labeled this approach "Participating." Finally, when a person is very experienced at their task, comfortable with doing it independently, and willing to take on the responsibility for it, the leader is still involved in some decisions and monitors progress but entrusts the process and responsibility to the person. This is "Delegating."

I have found this basic model very helpful for thinking about how associate staff members grow in competence in their work over time, and how supervisors need to be prepared to shift their style of leadership and supervision in light of the staff member's growth. A new staff member with little experience will need more direction, more frequent meetings to review progress and be reassured that things are going well, and more encouragement. As this same staff member continues to serve, she or he will gain understanding, skills, and confidence in doing the work, and the supervisor needs to become less directive and allow the staff member to take on more responsibility, but still have regular times for checking in and confirming that the tasks are being approached in the right way. As more experience is gained, more knowledge and skill acquired, and confidence grows, the supervisor needs to give more room and responsibility to the staff member, allowing him or her to make more decisions, with the supervisor continuing to have a strong supportive relationship. Finally, as the staff member is able to take on full responsibility for the various ministry tasks, true delegation can take place, with less frequent meetings needed, but still having good communication of what is going on in the ministry so the supervisor is able to respond if new challenges arise.

But, old habits die hard! We may tend to hang onto supervision styles that were helpful once, but no longer fit the "maturity" of the staff member we are supervising. This kind of problem is easier to see in another application of Hersey and Blanchard's theory—how our parenting styles need to change as our children grow and mature into fully functioning adults. This difficulty of our adapting our style to our children's growth in maturity may also be true of our leadership approaches with our associate staff who are growing in their capacity to take on more responsibility in their ministry areas. As staff members grow, our leadership and supervision approaches need to change, or we can end up stifling and frustrating them.

We asked the supervisors that we interviewed about this challenge, and we heard them describe how their approaches had to change not only with the experience of the staff member but also with the "ministry season" they were immersed in. Here are two examples:

> *Part of it's just meeting regularly. Just enforcing that. It depends on the role; for the guy who does our music and all that, we meet every week. For other people who do youth, it's every two weeks, and then we've got a couple guys that have been around for a long time, and with them it's once a month. You just have to schedule those, you have to make those happen, because if you don't then it's two months before you've really sat down and put the cards on the table saying, "This is going good, this isn't so good."*

> *The goal is about twice a month, I'm sitting down with them on more specific things that are related to their ministry and their personal development . . . and that changes depending on the season, so as we're ramping [up,] discipleship has its ebbs and flows. Worship part is pretty consistent throughout the year, so that's pretty steady. The family life guys have busy seasons and off seasons. As they're heading into busy seasons [I] usually want to spend more time with them, just on visionary planning. . . . The guys reporting to me are pretty high capacity guys, so it isn't a micromanaging thing most of the time. It's just making sure that they're processing, they're thinking through things right, that they're not overloading themselves or their teams. A bit more care, probably, than down to the micromanaging of details because they've been doing it for a while, and they're pretty capable.*

It is also important to check in and confirm if the supervision approach you are using is working well for this staff member, or if it may be assuming or presuming too much. I've been guilty of that in the past, assuming someone is capable and confident to handle the task, only to find out later that my more "hands off" approach made them feel very insecure. One pastor talks about realizing that he needs to consider the different needs of his associate staff members.

That's actually an important point, because I don't need a whole lot of direction. So if we talk about an idea about doing something, I could walk away and I could do it, or I'll say, "I've got it." I used to value that, and I just wanted for someone to just say that and walk away. And [I] probably looked down on people, I'm sure that came out somehow, if they needed a lot more specifics. That's the biggest difference is to be able to say: people are different, . . . and people need different things, and some people need more specifics.

With this important reminder about the need to adapt our supervision style to the growth and maturity of our associate staff members, we want to briefly share some recommendations in five areas that can help make your *One-on-Ones* both productive and encouraging for you and your associates.

Pursue regular, proactive interaction to build relationships, get on the same page in ministry approach, not just for problem solving or critique. *One-on-Ones* should not happen only when there is a problem to solve or behavior to correct. They need to be pursued on a regular basis to provide opportunity to build a strong work relationship, a common understanding of what is important and where ministries are heading, and the clarification of expectations by the supervisor and the associate staff member. These regular meetings are a simple way of investing in a strong work relationship. Three associate staff members share how important their regular *One-on-Ones* with their supervisors are for them, helping them gain confidence that they are heading in the right direction in their work.

My best supervising pastors meet weekly with me, willing to discuss and process all the aspects of my ministry area, plus bring me into their thoughts and ideas which helped me get a better sense how they worked so I could work under them better.

My supervising pastor (a youth pastor) consistently met with me about both the ministry that I was leading and my personal life. We spent time discussing vision and planning together. I was given freedom to work on my own, but my supervising pastor spent time helping me to debrief different ministry events.

My pastor did a good job of balancing between enough vision-casting and guidance on the front end, followed by plenty of space for me to work things out in my own way as the ministry begins to roll out. Then checking in regularly to see how things are going, rather than waiting for a crisis to emerge before stepping in.

When these kinds of meetings are not part of the regular schedule, they can quickly become a negative experience since they only happen when there are problems to correct. One supervisor reflected back on his own associate staff experience and the challenges that came when there were no regular *One-on-One* times with his supervisor.

. . . about two years ago we had a staff culture where, we had some staff and said okay, these are the people who report to you and if you need anything, get with them. So here's what would happen. You'd have somebody kind of tap on your door and say, "Can I see you for a second?" Would that be a real positive fun thing? No. You only get together with a report when something was wrong, when something went sideways. That was the only time because the assumption was, well, we're working on the other stuff kind of together, kind of fluidly throughout the week, . . . but you get the tap on the door, "Hey, could we sit down, could you meet me in my office?" That was always bad.

Take time for focused reviewing and planning. Many times, the *Regular Team Meeting* time is not the right time and place for extended discussion about one person's ministry area. Scheduling *One-on-Ones* allows the needed time for interaction without tying up other team members not impacted by the area under discussion. More detailed discussion is possible, tailoring this to the "job maturity" of the staff member. Even just asking how things went in any recent ministry activities opens the opportunity for reflection, review, troubleshooting, learning for the future. One supervisor, reflecting on his own experience as an associate staff member, shared,

The best thing my lead pastor has done is to simply follow up with me. He would intentionally go out of his way to ask, make suggestions, and follow through with asking how things went.

Another supervisor comments on how important his biweekly meetings are with his associate staff members, and how important it is for him to take notes so he can follow up well over time.

. . . having a bi-weekly meeting with direct reports is necessary for me because every other week we have that accountability, where they're going to come and bring their ministry projects and questions, but then I'm going to refer back to what we've talked about in previous meetings. I'm going to ask them questions, and if I didn't have that regularly scheduled meeting I would forget, honestly, because I take notes, not detailed notes, but just generic enough that I know we talked about this issue, or this volunteer, or this situation. What's the follow up on that? How's it going with that? That's been a discipline for me.

Take time for detailed assessment, sharing concerns and correction, troubleshooting, and encouragement as needed. *Regular Team Meetings* are not the place for correcting staff members or sharing major concerns with their ministry areas. That kind of interaction should be saved for private *One-on-One* times, not done in front of others. The kind of detailed ministry debriefing and assessment that allows concerns to surface and correction to be given needs to be done in *One-on-One* sessions. The opportunity to raise questions and concerns and have an open conversation is one of the advantages of regular *One-on-Ones*. When this is done, there needs to be an effort to affirm what you can and to help the staff member do self-assessment to see the challenges or problems that you are seeing. No one likes to be corrected, and a regular experience of encouragement on the job helps the recipient of correction know that you are "for" her or him. One of our supervisor interviewees shares how this was recently approached with one of their church associates:

> *I had a meeting with [name] last week, and there were certain parts where he was frustrated about some things, and there were some parts where I needed to clarify hey, I don't think how you're thinking about this is the complete picture. So I needed to kind of do a little correction, but I found myself saying a lot of things in preparation for that, to affirm him. So I think I saw this little thing go off in his eye that said oh okay I'm safe to hear the criticism. So I think I'm looking for that a little bit better now, that people feeling safe, that sense that that safety is there.*

Having regular times for *One-on-Ones* also allows issues to be raised in a timely manner, not letting too much time go by and problems grow. However, on occasion there may be a need to deal with something right away, and a history of healthy interaction together provides a good foundation for quickly addressing unexpected challenges that arise. One of our supervisors explained how they try to quickly respond to certain kinds of challenges.

> *If we see or hear or anything that we have concerns about, we try to address it right away. "Hey, this parent had this concern, it came to me, I encouraged them to go and talk to you, but I wanted to make sure they followed through and talked to you about it. If you need me to sit down and talk with you and the parent together," we have a few parents that are hyper over-protective. "If you need me to sit down, if you can't work it out, . . . Hey I noticed this isn't happening," or if there's kids wandering around in the parking lot when they're supposed to be in the worship center in your program, "How can you address that?" Try to sit down and address it right away. Go right to them.*

One-on-Ones allow us to give the individual attention that each team member needs, the right combination of direction, encouragement, assessment, and guidance. As time goes by, we have to continue to adapt our approach as our team members continue to learn and grow into their responsibilities.

Be sure to listen and invite their agenda. *One-on-Ones* are a great opportunity for the supervisor to learn what she or he needs to learn to have confidence that a particular area of ministry is headed in the right direction, and that the person leading that ministry is doing well. However, these kinds of meetings are not just for the supervisor's benefit, and we have to be careful that we do not dominate these meetings, working through our own agenda and then leaving. *One-on-Ones* provide an opportunity for us to listen to our associate staff members, to invite them to raise questions and concerns, to clarify things that are confusing, and to learn how we might better serve their needs in ministry and personally. The time should not be rushed, or it will tend to degenerate to being focused just on tasks. One supervisor was struggling to understand how he might better support the church's preschool director and learned that the first step was to simply listen.

> *But we had a preschool director who was trained and licensed and we had all these preschool teachers, trained and licensed. Even though I didn't feel as though I was doing anything, I would meet with the preschool director and I would listen. And that's to me a better way of supervising. Let me listen until I hear the need I can fill. I can encourage, I can approve, I can do all these things, but when I listen, . . . "Oh, you don't have somebody who makes good fliers." I can step in that area. I know somebody, now I can be involved.*

Some supervisors have a regular habit of getting together with their associate staff members in *One-on-Ones* without any agenda at all. Their goal is to learn so they can better understand how to supervise and support the person in his or her ministry. One supervisor shares their regular pattern and approach, and what they hope to gain from it.

> *Then I usually am off to lunch with somebody, but in the afternoon I try to circle around to each person's office and sit down and listen, and do they have stuff we need to touch base on? It's just seeing how they're doing and interacting on what they would want to talk about.*

Whether you have the time for this kind of approach or not, make sure that at least a part of your time in your *One-on-Ones* is spent actively listening to your associate staff members, inviting them to bring up and discuss what is important and helpful for them.

Most important: make prayer together a priority. Finally, as personal and ministry concerns are shared, or joys and accomplishments noted, take time together to pray for the ministry your associate is invested in, and for your associate. Allow your associate to pray for you and for your ministry. Model dependence on God and make it a priority in your times together. This is one of the strongest forms of encouragement we can offer our associate staff members. Having times of prayer together lends credibility when you say that you are praying for her or him when you are apart. Pursue God's grace, wisdom, and strength together. As one associate staff member shares,

> *Taking time to pray together helps me to not get too task-oriented. Praying together gives me a view of his faith and perspective on what God is doing in our ministry.*

TWO FINAL ISSUES TO CONSIDER

Before closing out this chapter, there are two additional items we would like to comment on that you may find helpful.

Technology Use for Communication. Good communication is the primary goal of face-to-face meetings of all kinds. Contemporary technology allows us to supplement our face-to-face gatherings with quick communication on the go. While tools such as texting, e-mails, Facebook, Skype, and tweets can increase our flow of information and help with rapid decision making, there are two challenges that need to be considered. The first is that the variety of communication methods now available can be challenging if everyone on staff is not using and regularly checking the same ones. It would be good to sit down together and identify which methods you will all use, and make sure that you regularly check those that you identify. One supervising pastor describes this challenge at their church:

> . . . *we're finding it harder and harder to communicate with people now that we have more and more different ways. It's actually harder because some people text, some people don't e-mail but they text, or some people don't get on Facebook, some people do this, some do that. We tell our staff that you need to be checking your e-mail every 24–48 hours and you need to get back to people within 24 hours. You need to check your voicemails . . . we can't have one or two ways we communicate. We need to be open to at least three to four different common ways people communicate. That is a big challenge.*

Open-Door Policy. In an effort to communicate to their associate staff that they are approachable, many supervisors say that they have an "open-door policy." Their desire is to reassure their associate staff that they can come to them with questions and concerns and not wait until the next planned meeting. However, if a staff member comes at a time when the supervisor is absorbed in a challenging task and the supervisor, through body language, communicates that this is not a good time to talk, it can make the associate feel hesitant to come again. One very simple solution to consider is to make your "open-door" policy a literal one. My senior pastor at our church in Maine did this. When the door to his office was open, he was available to talk with anyone as needed. However, when the door was closed, we knew not to interrupt him unless it was an emergency. This simple solution let us approach him with confidence that he was ready and available to listen and talk, and it let us know when to leave him alone. You may find that something like this, or a simple sign on the door, will help your staff as well.

TAKING INVENTORY

Like the previous chapters, we've put together some questions for personal reflection, and others for discussion with your associate staff members. Don't try to address all of them, but look through these and identify those you think would be most beneficial to give attention to. Find a time soon to work through them on your own, or together. It is worth the investment to make your *Occasional Team Gatherings* and *One-on-Ones* a great investment.

Occasional Team Gatherings

Spiritual Retreats

Leader: How long has it been since your ministry team shared a spiritual retreat together? From what you see across your team, would this be a good thing to pursue soon? What opportunities are available nearby to do this as a one-day experience, or as an overnight? Can you get approval to invest time and funds in doing this together?

Together: (If you have had a retreat together) What did you appreciate about our last retreat together? If we could do another one soon, what do you think would be beneficial for us as a team?

(If you have *not* had a retreat together before) If we were able to get some time away together for a spiritual retreat, what do you think would be beneficial for us as a team? Given the workload you are carrying, when do things open up so that we might consider doing this together?

Planning Retreats

Leader: If you have had a planning retreat together in the past, what aspects were most beneficial to you personally, and to the group? Given the work ahead for your team, do you think a one-day or overnight planning retreat would be beneficial? If so, what do you think would be most important to accomplish in this kind of time away? What opportunities are there to do this without a high cost?

Together: As you look at the ministry ahead over the next several months, do you think we need a planning retreat away together for a day or more? If so, what would you hope we could accomplish in this time together? How would this be beneficial to you and your ministry area(s)?

Conferences & Seminars

Leader: If you have gone to a conference with some of your staff in the past, what was most beneficial about that experience? How did you debrief the event together? Was there anything that made you wonder if this was a good investment of time and funds? What kind of training event would you like to take your team to if you could? What opportunities are there in your area over the coming year? Might your ministerial group be interested in working together on an event to benefit all of your pastoral staff members?

Together: (If you have been to a conference together with other staff members) How beneficial was it to go to that event together? What did we do after the event that helped you process what you learned? Was there anything you wish we had done as a follow-up to that event? What kind of training event do you think we might all benefit from, given where we are in our ministry efforts?

(If you have *not* gone to a conference with other staff members): What kind of training event do you think we might all benefit from participating in? How would it be of help to you personally? Why do you think it could be beneficial for us as a group?

Socials & Celebrations

Leader: Looking back over the last six to twelve months, where have you built in times for social events with your staff (and with their spouses or families)? What have you celebrated together? Does your group have a good pattern of "time off task" for fellowship and celebration? Looking ahead, where might there be opportunities for some informal times together to foster a growing fellowship? What would be worth celebrating together? Whose help will you need to organize these kinds of events?

Together: Which fellowship times have we had in the past that you really enjoyed? Are we taking enough time together "off task" for fun and fellowship together? If we could, what would you like to see us do together for fun? What might your spouses and families enjoy doing together?

One-on-One Meetings

Tailoring Your One-on-Ones

Leader: As you consider the "job maturity" of each of your associate staff members, how much direction, encouragement, and checking in do you see them needing? Are there patterns of supervision you have used up to now that need to begin to change in light of their growing experience and accountability? Are there "seasons" to their workflow where more or less checking in is needed? Consider discussing this with your associate staff members.

With Each Staff Member: As you think about the ways I have tried to supervise and support you over the last several months, when we have met together one-on-one, what have you most appreciated from me? Given your growth on the job over the last few months/years, is there anything you feel you need more of, or less of, from me? How might we adapt our meeting times to make them more beneficial for you?

Proactive Interaction

Leader: Do you find yourself having regular, proactive conversations with each of your staff members, or do you tend to wait until there is an issue or problem before you find time to meet with them? How are you using your time with each staff member to build a strong working relationship together? What might be beneficial to start doing when you meet?

With Each Staff Member: Are we getting together one-on-one often enough to be of most help to you? What would be good for us to do when we meet so that this time is most constructive for you?

Focused Reviewing and Planning: Debriefing, Concerns and Correction, Troubleshooting, Encouragement

Leader: In what ways are you using your time together one-on-one to help your associate staff members in debriefing their ministry efforts? Are you using these personal meetings for voicing any concerns or providing any correction? How are you preparing the ground for this kind of critique? In what ways are you communicating that you are "for" the staff member, and value her or his ministry? What kind of encouragement do you think each of your associates needs? Have you seen any change in what they need over the last few months?

With Each Staff Member: When we meet to debrief recent ministry events, what can I do that would be of help to you in your own assessment efforts? When I have raised concerns or offered correction in the past, have you felt my support in what I've said, or mainly my disapproval? How might I do a better job of affirming you even when there may be areas to work on?

Listening and Inviting Their Agenda

Leader: When you meet one-on-one with each staff member, do you tend to dominate the agenda? How are you inviting the staff member to raise her or his own questions and concerns? Are you somehow communicating that you are in a hurry, possibly shutting down their ability to initiate conversation on new issues? How do you think they would score you regarding your "active listening" skills?

With Each Staff Member: When we meet together, do you feel the freedom to raise your own questions or concerns, or does it seem as though I'm too focused on my own agenda and not creating space for you to bring up your own agenda? How am I doing at listening to you? How might I do a better job at this?

Prayer Together

Leader: When you meet one-on-one with each staff member, do you make sure that you pray for him or her before you leave? Do you invite that person to pray for something of concern to you? If this has not been part of your interaction, how might you initiate it?

With Each Staff Member: When we meet together, how might I support you best in prayer? What would you value in our prayer time together?

Technology Use for Communication

Leader: Are you seeing any challenges in communicating well at a distance among the staff? Are there too many "personal preferences" among the staff to find a consistent method for immediate communication and also for interaction that is less time sensitive? What are your own preferences?

With Each Staff Member: Have you had difficulties reaching anyone on staff when needed, or getting a response in a timely manner? What technologies do you prefer to use? What communication technologies might be good for all of us to use so we can count on reaching each other and getting a timely response?

Communicating Availability

Leader: What have you tried to communicate to your associate staff about your availability? What challenges have you seen in carrying that out over time? What might help your associate staff know when you really need to not be disturbed and when you are available if they want to talk?

With Each Staff Member: When you have come to me to talk, has it generally been clear to you when I am really available, or has it been awkward, hard to know if you are interrupting me or not?

Following Up: In light of what I have considered and/or we have discussed above, what needs to be given priority and addressed in the near future? What is important but can wait a while before we address it? When and where will these items be followed up on?

Chapter Five

Facilitating and Supporting the Ministry of Your Associate Staff

Kevin E. Lawson

As we began this book, we talked about how supervising others in ministry requires looking through bifocal lenses, with one lens focused on ensuring that the ministry is being done well and the other focused on the well-being of those doing the ministry. In this chapter, we're going to give attention to ways of facilitating and supporting the ministry efforts of your associate staff colleagues. The next chapter will focus on how to support your associate staff members in the midst of their ministry demands.

Let me start off with a question. What produces satisfaction for you in your ministry efforts? Is it seeing increased attendance, or increased giving, or receiving a lot of positive feedback? These are nice when they happen but on their own probably don't lead to a deep sense of satisfaction in ministry. For me, when I served as an associate staff member, satisfaction came when I knew what I needed to do, had the resources to carry it out, and was able to see good results over time. I didn't necessarily need a lot of praise or affirmation for my work from others, but it meant a lot when I was able to see that the ministry that I valued was going well, and I could see how my investment of time was bearing good fruit in the lives of others. More than anything else, I wanted the ministry areas that I was entrusted with to not just run smoothly but also have a positive impact in the lives of those who participated in them.

We believe that for many associate staff members, the best way to help them find deep satisfaction in their ministry is to provide them with the resources and support needed to allow their ministry areas to flourish. This is what they care about and what they feel called to invest themselves in, and when they see their ministry areas going well and having the desired impact in the lives of those who participate, it leads to a deep sense of fulfillment and makes all the sweat and long hours worthwhile.

In this chapter, we want to look at the ways that you, as a ministry supervisor, can provide the kind of practical support (table 5.1) your associate staff members need to help them do their jobs well and see good results from their efforts.

KEEPING UP WITHOUT HOVERING

The first practice that is important for supporting the ministry of your associate staff members is simply to keep up on what is happening in their areas of ministry. This falls under the *Regular Team Meetings* and *One-on-Ones* that we talked about in chapters 3 and 4. Keeping up on what is happening is important because it reinforces the value of that area of ministry, shows your concern and desire to understand what is happening, and helps you as a supervisor have peace of mind regarding that ministry area. It also allows issues to be raised and addressed before they become more problematic. This does not always require formal meetings but can be done with brief conversations in the hall or over a coffee. Two of the associate staff members we heard from describe how they felt supported in this way:

I never felt more supported in my ministry than when my supervising pastor asked how things were going. Though too few and far between, I do remember sitting in my supervising pastor's office and being asked how my ministry was going. It was great having him share some good feedback and/or concerns, and especially when our time ended with him praying for me.

My pastor did a good job of balancing between enough vision-casting and guidance on the front end, followed by plenty of space for me to work things out in my own way as the ministry begins to roll out. Then checking in regularly to see how things are going, rather than waiting for a crisis to emerge before stepping in.

Table 5.1.   Five Positive Practices for Supporting Your Associate Ministry Staff

Keeping up without hovering

Ensuring they have the needed resources

Coordinating with other ministries

Developing congregational and lay leader support

Backing them up as needed

Another way of keeping up on what is happening in the various ministries your associate staff supervise is to occasionally take time to visit them in action. Your presence there, even for a few minutes, communicates the value you place on that area of ministry and your desire to be a support. It also allows you to see firsthand some of the good things happening and some things that may be good to talk about together later. The goal is to make the visit a supportive experience, not an evaluation. Express appreciation to those working alongside your associate staff member, pray with them, make it clear how important this ministry area is to your church. This is affirmed strongly by several of the associate staff members in our study.

> *Another thing that was supportive was when he would visit our meetings from time to time. It was always good to see that he was interested in what we were doing.*

> *My supervising pastor was present at some events. I never felt like I was being evaluated, since he communicated support to me through constructive criticism and warm friendship. When I had difficulties, we addressed them together. I knew that I had an advisor that would support me in challenges. For instance, one family was unhappy with some of the kids attending youth group. I met with my supervising pastor, and we brainstormed different ways to address their concerns.*

> *None of them came and stood in the back with a clipboard, but through passing by, conversations with other leaders, parents and students, they had a good sense of what was going on, and when I talked with them, it was apparent.*

But one of the challenges in doing this is to not come across as "looking over their shoulders" as if you do not trust them. This can be addressed partly by how often you initiate checking in (not too frequently), the level of detail in the questions you ask (keep it more general), and the affirmation you give (as much as you can). It can also help to make yourself available for your associate staff members to reach out to as they feel the need, not just waiting for you to check in. We talked about this at the end of chapter 4. Knowing that they can come to you as needed helps them feel supported as they work through the challenges of their ministry efforts. One associate staff member expresses it this way:

> *One [thing] that he did that was very helpful was that he made himself available to me, always answering my calls despite maintaining a very busy schedule himself. He encouraged me to call with any questions or serious issues, and this proved invaluable to me as I had to confront some very challenging sin issues in the ministry almost at the outset.*

ENSURING THEY HAVE THE
NEEDED RESOURCES

It seems like a no-brainer to say that if you want to support the ministry efforts of your associate staff members, you need to ensure that they have the resources they need to get their work done well. While I hope this does not come as a surprise, as supervisors we don't always appreciate some of the challenges that associate staff members have getting the needed resources and how we might play a significant role in helping them do so.

In Carl Larson and Frank LaFasto's book *Teamwork: What Must Go Right, What Can Go Wrong*,[1] which reports on their groundbreaking research on effective teams, the authors describe how good team leaders think about the resources their team members need and find ways to secure those resources, sometimes from others outside the immediate team setting. As a pastor in your church you will often be aware of people who have the ability to assist with various needs and who may have an interest in helping out with a particular event or effort. You have different connections and may be able to rally support for an associate staff member's ministry. You may also be able to help round up scarce resources for your associate staff members. Take time to find out what they need, and together determine what they can secure on their own and where having your involvement may be of help. Sometimes it is a matter of recognizing where there is a roadblock that needs your help to be removed, perhaps credibility, or permission for something new. One of our supervisors described it this way:

> . . . *being clear on what their job is, what it is we're really asking them to do, and then what the win looks like for their role. And then having clear expectations of what are the key priorities, and checking in on those. I thought that was one of my biggest jobs, was to remove organizational roadblocks, and try to get the resources that person needed.*

Another associate staff member described how important his supervising pastor's connections were for a ministry initiative.

> *He entrusted me with a lot of authority and supported my decisions. He explained the vision for the ministry, and then he helped me figure out how to pursue that. One way this looked practically was leaning on his connections with other people in the church to get a response.*

Another of our supervising pastors described how they attempt to keep up on the ministry needs of their associate staff while providing the needed freedom to give leadership to their ministry areas and proper accountability for results.

Well, just recently we've gone through and reviewed all our job descriptions so we know who is doing what. . . . And then on a probably semi-annual basis he sits down and says in view of the things we talked about last time, how's progress? Is your budget commensurate with ministry advancements and needs? That sort of practical nuts and bolts, what do we need and what do we get for what we gave?

Sometimes associate staff can feel a bit shy about asking for more resources, so you need to have the kind of open conversations that encourage honest discussions of areas of need. Showing that you are interested and willing to help where you can makes a big difference. All of these examples show how at times you can have an important role in ensuring that your associate staff members have what they need to do their ministry well.

COORDINATING WITH OTHER MINISTRIES

Sometimes associate staff members can feel as though they are in competition with each other for scarce resources. This can commonly be experienced in the areas of funding, calendaring, and personnel recruitment. An active church that is trying to staff a wide range of ministries can inadvertently create competition among staff for church members to serve in ministry leadership roles. The church calendar and facilities can easily become a battleground for ministry leaders trying to do their best to plan ahead. Budgets only go so far, and it can be easy to consider your ministry area more important and worthy of additional funding than another staff member's. These kinds of challenges are why developing a strong sense of being a ministry team is so important (reread chapter 2). When this is not handled well, associate staff report the impact on their ministries and the discouragement it can produce.

When my supervising pastor took one of my staff or core members from English ministry that I depend on to fulfill the need of Korean ministry, I felt unsupported as I was also lacking in leaders, and any leader that rose out of the ministry seemed to have been snatched up by the supervising pastor. I know the intention is not there and [I] fully understand the need of it, but as an associate, that's how it felt.

In one case where I was a college pastor in a mostly white church, the church was having financial difficulties. The Christian ed. pastor, my supervisor, kept taking money out of my budget. In retrospect, I am not even sure if it was legal. I was trying to recruit leaders from the young people who returned to the church to check out the college ministry but only found that other staff persons had recruited them behind my back. So it was a case of sheep stealing within the same church among different ministries.

To support each of your associate staff members, it is important that you assist them in finding ways to coordinate their ministry efforts with one another. *Regular Team Meetings* can be the place to look at plans for the future and the implications they may have for personnel needs, budget, and facilities use. Annual or semiannual planning meetings may also help with this, allowing longer-term planning to be discussed together so staff members can focus on how to help one another with their ministry plans instead of feeling like competitors (see chapter 3). Your leadership in setting policies and procedures for personnel recruitment, facilities scheduling, and new budget requests can create a better work environment with less stress felt by staff members about their ability to secure what their ministry area needs. Also, how you respond to staff members when these procedures and policies are violated (and they will be at times) is important for maintaining an environment of both grace and accountability. Violations cannot be ignored without creating ill will among other staff. There may be times when forgiveness will need to be asked for and given, and policies and procedures revisited and reaffirmed. You are in the best position to help prevent these kinds of problem situations from occurring and helping your staff navigate them if they do.

DEVELOPING CONGREGATIONAL AND LAY LEADER SUPPORT

One of the best gifts we can give to our associate staff members is to find ways to affirm the importance of their ministry areas with the congregation and lay leaders and to promote their support for those ministries. As a supervising pastor, you are often in settings where you have an opportunity to say a word to your congregation that can make a difference in how various ministries are perceived, particularly new initiatives. Your public support builds credibility for the ministry effort, raising its value in the eyes of your congregation and increasing support for these efforts. One associate staff member describes what he saw as a lack of support and its impact.

> *I think that a lack of promotion from the pulpit might have affected the level (of) participation I saw in my ministry. I've seen that preachers have tremendous influence over the culture of the church. If they don't regularly endorse the church's ministry teams, the congregants tend to lose awareness.*

Taking time to highlight upcoming events or needs in support of the ministries your associate staff supervise is always appreciated and can pay big dividends in congregational awareness, support, and involvement.

It is also important for a ministry supervisor to do what she or he can to develop lay leaders' awareness of associate staff members' ministry areas and confidence in their leadership. This should be a mixture of support for the ministry area and support for the staff member leading that ministry. When done well, this expands the number of people in the church who are showing interest in your staff members' ministry areas, asking how they are doing, and expressing support for their efforts. There are a number of ways that this can be done.

In church settings where the supervising pastor meets with the church board but the associate staff members do not, the supervisor needs to represent the staff well and build support for their ministries. One supervising pastor shares the importance of this:

> . . . I try to make sure our lay leaders know as much as possible what the paid staff, the pastoral staff are doing. Make sure they know what we're doing and try to be transparent as possible about the work that we're doing. I feel that it's my job to advertise the work of our staff, especially the people I'm supervising. Trying to make sure that all the behind the scenes stuff that happens, we talk about that, and people are aware of that.

In these kinds of contexts, when a supervisor is aware that there may be questions or concerns about new initiative changes in a ministry area, he or she needs to proactively talk with church leaders about the coming changes, providing a clear rationale and answering questions. The supervisor's role as "ambassador" for his or her associate staff members is critical in maintaining a supportive environment. One associate staff member shares how important this was for him in the past.

> He [supervisor] informed the board and trusted me with executing new ministries. I sensed a protection and experienced how he "ran interference" and took care to communicate what our team was doing to the board.

Where possible, there can be great value in having associate staff members attend at least a part of a board meeting to share personally what is happening in their ministry areas. One senior pastor explains why he makes this a priority:

> . . . another thing we do is we invite the staff into the elder meetings, not for the whole meeting, but invite them in, especially if they want to report on something in their ministry. Rather than me coming in and being the voice for that staff person, no, you come in, you talk about how excited you are about VBS, or youth camp, or the new carpet we're getting, or whatever the situation is, and have them have that access, because it's theirs. It's their victory. It's their ministry. And that allows the elders to support and encourage them because it's not me reporting for them.

In settings where associate staff members also attend board meetings, supervisors still have a role to play in speaking words of affirmation regarding staff members' ideas and ministry efforts. This can go a long way in building both a sense of confidence on the part of the staff member and a spirit of support and appreciation by the board members. Empowering staff members in front of church leaders builds credibility, as expressed by this associate staff member.

> *He gave me a good amount of freedom to manage the ministry and empowered me in front of the leadership and the church verbally. Let's say at leadership meeting, the pastor would verbally recognize my gifting publicly. Not once, not twice, but many times.*

Another way that some supervising pastors have sought to build support by church elders for staff members and their ministries has been to match up an elder with an associate staff member for more personal interaction and support. Where this can be done and monitored to ensure staff members are receiving benefits from this, it can do a lot to increase the sense of support associate staff members feel. After discussing some of the challenges in doing this, one supervising pastor expresses what he would like to see.

> *I think one elder could be assigned to each ministry each year. Just to partner with that ministry and maybe connect in with the leader of the ministry, and show up to one or two things. They don't need to come to a whole lot, but just to have a presence and a prayer support and an encouragement.*

However, it is easy to set something like this up, only to have it fade because people are busy. Try it for short periods of time, and remind the lay leaders of what you are asking of them. Make sure it is carried out well, or the associate staff members may feel discouraged.

All of these responses are ways to build support by members of the congregation and the church's lay leadership for the ministry areas and efforts of your associate staff. These are worth investing in to expand the support your staff feel for their ministries.

BACKING THEM UP AS NEEDED

The devastating experiences that some associate staff members have reported are the times when there was a criticism or conflict in their ministry, and their supervising pastor did not come to them to sort it out but too quickly sided with those voicing the concern. One associate staff member shares this experience.

> *[Supervisors] did not have my back in difficult situations with other staff.*
> *Would allow staff and leaders to come to them [with] issues rather than point*
> *them first to me. In the two mega-churches I worked in there was either no*
> *annual review process or it was poorly done. Always felt blindsided by nega-*
> *tive input. Relationship broke down and communication became almost non-*
> *existent. Felt isolated and unsupported.*

A supervising pastor who used to be a youth pastor reflects on the impact of this kind of experience when it happens with parents and the senior pastor.

> *Youth pastors just get hung if the senior isn't clear that they need some space*
> *to operate. If a parent complains, and the senior sides with the parents and*
> *says he can't figure out why the youth pastor would be that stupid, either; . . .*
> *you're never recovering from that, because the guy's . . . nobody knows he has*
> *any clout.*

No one wants to undermine the leadership of those he or she supervises, but sometimes when a congregational member or leader comes with a full head of steam, it can be difficult to remain neutral and encourage a careful review that involves the associate staff member in an appropriate way. So it is important that as supervisors, you have thought through how you want to handle these "worst-case scenarios" and talk it through with your associate staff so you are all in agreement on expectations. As a starting point, has the person with the grievance talked with the associate staff member about it, or has she or he avoided that and gone straight to the supervisor? Direct conversation should be encouraged, allowing the opportunity for misunderstandings to be clarified, wrong actions to be repented for, and reconciliation to happen. If the results of that process are not satisfactory, then involving the supervisor may be the appropriate next step, but it needs discussion with the associate staff member.

If you believe in your staff, it is important to communicate that and reassure them that you will support them in conflict situations or in times of failure. One supervising pastor explains how he works through this with his associate staff members.

> *I tell my staff, not every day, but on a regular basis . . . that if they blow it, if*
> *they do something wrong or make a mistake, I will never abandon them in*
> *public or in front of those who are giving them grief for the failure, or to the*
> *boards. If they really did blow it, and it was just dumb, we will talk behind*
> *closed doors one-on-one, and I will deal with the issue, basically say don't*
> *ever do that again type stuff. They know I will not stab them in the back.*

If failures and conflicts continue, there may come a time when support can no longer be given, but this is a matter for private conversation, not public. We'll address this kind of issue in chapter 7. For now, our bias needs to be *for* our associate staff members, and it has to be backed up with how we respond in support of them when complaints come.

A MAJOR TRAP TO AVOID: MICROMANAGEMENT

In the last part of this chapter, we want to focus attention on the number-one concern raised by associate staff members when they were asked about what their supervisors did that hindered their ability to do their ministry well. The overwhelmingly most common response was a sense of being "micromanaged." This relates to the discussion we had in chapter 4 on situational leadership, and it needs more careful consideration. Let's begin by looking at this issue in another common context—parenting.

Mick and I are both parents of grown children. During the years that mine were growing up and still living at home, I used to talk about how my goal was to not "raise children," but to "raise adults." By this I meant that I wanted and expected them to grow and take on more responsibility for themselves and be able to exercise wise judgment as they learned along the way. This was an admirable goal, and my children have done this well, but in all honesty, it was a challenge to figure out how to parent them as they were growing into adulthood. I think that too often I would not really trust them with some plans or decisions because I would be remembering some time in the past when they showed bad judgment or forgot something important, which led me to ask them a lot of questions about their plans or to remind them of things I thought were important that they may not have thought of. Sometimes I think I just fell back on parenting habits of the past, not realizing that my children were growing and no longer needed that same level of guidance. I suspect that many times, my children felt that my questioning was too much like a "grilling," and that it revealed a real lack of trust in them. What complicated this even more was that each of my three children matured in different ways at different rates. What I did with one of them was not necessarily best for another one. For me, parenting became a challenging art, and I was not always the best artist, but I tried hard to learn what each of them would benefit from most.

Supervising associate staff members has many similarities with parenting. In each case, our goal is to raise up people who are able to take on responsibilities of life and ministry and be able to exercise good judgment in doing so. Also in each case, they may start off needing a bit of guidance and only over time be able to carry out their work independently. In each case, we, the parents/supervisors, need to be able to adapt our guidance and support patterns to what they will most benefit from. And, in each case, old supervision habits, and remembering times of past failures, may make it hard for us to release them, trusting that they will be up to the current challenge.

One more challenge should be noted. It is much easier to see other parents as "helicopter parents," and other ministry supervisors as "micromanaging," than to see it in ourselves. We have "reasons" for our actions, and we can justify to ourselves why we have to be more involved in giving guidance right now. It really is hard to see this in ourselves, and many supervising pastors would be surprised to hear how some of their actions are perceived more as "micromanaging" than as helpful guidance and support.

It may help to start with simply listening to a few of the associate staff members who write about how the perceived micromanagement of their supervisors negatively impacted them in their ministries. As you read below, consider if any of these things might be said of your interaction with your associate staff.

Sometimes [supervisor] would micro-manage me. Told me what to do instead of allowing me to come up with my own plans. Would be a bit overwhelming. Could sometimes nag and felt more like a parent than a supporting pastor.

Nothing hindered my taking responsibility more than when my supervising pastor made decisions that affected my ministry without consulting, or speaking, with me first.

I once worked with a supervising pastor that was micro-managing. It gave me the impression that I couldn't be trusted, and it also restricted me from developing my own ministry style and leadership. There was also a clear "I am your supervisor and you are younger than me" distinction that made me feel that I just had to perform a job (and not particularly encouraged to grow in ministry skills, vision, or values).

I recall one supervisor that was so far into the weeds, he was even instructing a volunteer and I on the proper way to plug in an extension cord. Overly task oriented leadership, like drilling into the smallest details on people, becomes pretty exhausting.

Negligence and micro-managing have both made ministry more difficult. I've had very different experiences. With one pastor, I would spend many hours developing a plan and then never have a chance to discuss it with him. With another pastor, I would spend many hours developing a plan and then he, in our meeting and without much prior prayer or thought, would completely alter the plan. Both actions are demoralizing. I have always wanted to start an internship which would eventually morph into a training school. Our lead pastor has a similar vision. He asked me to write up a plan for it and a timeline. I spent 10–15 hours doing just that. I showed up to our meeting and he had spent an hour writing his own plan. We didn't talk about mine, even though I would be heading up the ministry and giving it vision.

In addition, a couple of the supervising pastors we interviewed also reflect on this challenge among supervisors and what causes us to fail at times by either micromanaging or neglecting.

> *I'd say probably the biggest thing that I see pastors fail at, especially those that go from small churches on through . . . you know, small, medium, large, mega . . . is they can't resist the urge to micromanage. And I've heard that again and again from associate staff who say . . . "He's always looking over my shoulder, he never releases ministry to me, he has a hard time delegating. I feel like a glorified volunteer." So they express concerns of, "I'm called, I'm gifted, I was hired, and yet I'm on a four-foot chain, and he just can't release me."*

> *I think I left people too unattended. Again that delicate balance is when they don't have a stronger leadership, they tend to go their own way and own path. That happens more when I'm in a season of stress, or personally out of balance, or I've got so many other things on my plate that I don't have the time, and I think "they're going to be fine." But what happens is people really do need leadership, even if they've been there for a length of time. They need you to step in, they need you to know what's going on, so you have to step back in for seasons, step back out for seasons.*

Recognizing the challenges of fitting our supervision style to the experience and job maturity of those we supervise, we have identified several practical tips that can help you avoid being a micromanager with those you supervise (table 5.2).

Approach Supervision As an Art, Not a Science

We can expect that those we supervise will need different supervision styles from us, so we shouldn't lock into one approach for everyone, or maintain one approach with someone too long over time without checking to see if it is

---

Table 5.2.   Seven Practical Tips for Avoiding Micromanagement and Neglect

Approach supervision as an art, not a science

Continually check in for what is needed and appreciated

Invite new ideas and allow the freedom to fail

Debrief ministry events to learn from failures and challenges

Forget past failures and expect real learning

Provide new stretching experiences

Affirm wherever possible

helping him or her. One supervisor reflects on the differences seen in the associate staff he supervises.

> *And I think that what we've learned more is that some people need a longer time with a shorter leash, and some people they need a long leash to begin with, that's the way that they learn. Some people need to learn by making some mistakes, [for] some people an early mistake devastates their career and they just can't recover from that. . . . We know that there's going to be failure there, and we want to make sure we communicate that we have a tolerance for failure, as long as people are learning from those mistakes.*

As an art, we won't always get it right, but we need to make the effort to see those we supervise as growing individuals. Our goal is to adapt our supervision over time to where eventually the staff member is able to function well on his or her own, needing minimal input from us, but always appreciating our support.

Continually Check In for What Is Needed and Appreciated

One of the great benefits of regular *One-on-Ones* is that they give us an opportunity to check in and see how the ministry is going and how our supervision approach may be helping or hindering. Micromanagement is not the only danger. Sometimes we may trust a staff member and feel that he or she can handle a new assignment, but our "hands-off" approach may be perceived as neglect and a lack of support. I know that I have been guilty of this, and I was surprised when I later learned how discouraging that experience was for the person I supervised. I suspect that we were not meeting often enough for me to catch this, and the person wanted to show his capability and felt awkward about asking for more help. That is why it is important to have these regular times of interaction. One associate staff member reflects on his experiences and what works best for him.

> *I've had both positive and negative experiences. . . . I think the challenge overseeing pastors have is balancing intervention with freedom. I've had both negligence and micromanaging. Neither allowed me to grow. In those seasons in which I'm given freedom to chart a course and also accountability to someone more experienced than myself, I feel supported.*

So, at your one-on-one sessions, have the courage to ask if your guidance is appreciated or if there are things you are doing that are beginning to feel like micromanagement or neglect. Admitting that you recognize that these are possibilities, and things that you want to avoid, may open up good dialogue about where your guidance is best needed and appreciated. This will also allow you to see growth over time and where some of your questions and guidance is no longer needed because the person owns that aspect of their work well.

Invite New Ideas and Allow the Freedom to Fail

One hard question we need to face as supervisors is how we will respond when our associate staff member comes to us with an idea for a ministry that is not how we would normally approach it. Are we open to these new ideas and willing to allow the staff member to shape the ministry in new ways, as long as it fits in with the DNA of our church, or are we secretly wanting them to lead the ministry the way we would if we were in charge of it? It can be easy to hang onto past ways of doing things and not be open to innovative ideas our associate staff members develop. One supervisor explains how he tried to both be open to new ideas and to give guidance with one of his staff.

> We had a younger guy who had been on staff at campus crusade, at least that's what they called it at the time, and he took leadership of our small groups. He had some new ideas about how we were going to train leaders, and so we really did let him run with that. I do think when you're giving someone that's not as experienced something new, it does mean you have to be willing to come alongside them a little more often to provide some coaching and kind of keep them between the guardrails. I remember I would meet with [name] regularly to review what he was thinking, the kind of materials he was developing, but it was his, he owned it, he really crafted the framework of it. I just tried to guide him a little bit along the way, inject some of what I thought was core DNA that he wanted our small groups leaders to get, but he was the hero.

But there is a risk in being open to new ideas and entrusting them to another staff member. There may be challenges and failures in that ministry effort. For those of us who like to play it safe, or like to be in control of things, this can be extremely hard. However, part of our staff members' growing into their responsibilities is to take risks and learn from the results. One supervisor reflects on the fear of failure and how supervisors need to respond.

> The senior pastors sometimes fear "what if I delegate and they fail? Then it's going to come back on me and I'm going to have people giving me grief." But if they fail, they're going to learn from that, and if they've got two brain cells to rub together, they'll probably avoid that mistake if you allow them the freedom to fail. I tell that to people on the staff all the time, "You have the freedom to fail, as long as you learn from it." If you don't learn from it, then we've got problems. You also have the freedom to succeed, which some people can handle failure better than the success.

This leads us to the next two points—how we can respond well when failure occurs.

Debrief Ministry Events to Learn from Failures and Challenges

One of the great benefits of regularly debriefing ministry activities and events with our associate staff is that these conversations can become great ways to draw out reflection and learning, setting the stage for more effective ministry in the future. This is not just about addressing big failures but about learning from what went well and what could have been done better. One of our supervisors shares some examples of how she goes about this with her associate staff in her debriefings with them.

> *I'll give feedback on what I observed. They've gone forward and done the meeting and planned the meeting without my direct micromanagement, and then what I'll do on the backside is say, "I really love this that and the other. I would have never even thought of that, that was phenomenal, your gifts are really shown here. Did you notice this little hiccup over here?" Or actually I'll ask them, "Tell me your feedback, what did you think went right, what went wrong?" And then it allows me the opportunity to say "Yeah, I noticed that too," or "Hey, this I would have done differently." And I try to do way more on the positive, but when I'm present and when I help evaluate on the backend, and get their own feedback, I find that they self lead and self teach if they're asked the question. And then you step forward from that and help them. The next time they've got that in their mind and they're going to take that. And so it's less for me.*

Regular debriefings are a key to catching teachable moments, inviting their reflection, and helping them chart better courses for the future. Inviting them to debrief first can allow you to see what they are already aware of and do not need you to point out. It can also help you see where they may have a blind spot and need some guidance to understand better.

Forget Past Failures and Expect Real Learning

One of the challenges we have when an associate staff member has failed in some aspect of ministry leadership, and we've debriefed about it, is to then leave that failure in the past and expect that he or she will learn from that experience and not make the same mistake again. I think that the natural tendency is to be alert to those same issues in the future and to remind the staff member of how important it is to make sure this is addressed better next time. Again, thinking about my parenting experiences can be helpful here. Too many times, I would remember some past error of judgment, or forgetting something important, and I could not resist checking on those things the next time my child was in a similar situation. We had already talked about it when it first happened, and I knew my child understood how important that was for the future, yet I somehow could not trust him or her to do it right the next time. I'm sure that created frustration for my children when I did that.

It takes discipline to let go of past failures and trust that real learning has occurred. As a supervisor, expressing your expectation and confidence that the errors of the past will be addressed in the future can allow your staff members to later demonstrate how they have grown and learned. Giving them that opportunity allows you to then affirm where they have improved, building their confidence in their ability to grow into the ministry well over time. Ask God to help you let go of the failures and your disappointments of the past to allow your staff the room they need to grow. It may also help for you to recall and share some of your own ministry failures, modeling humility and God's grace in your life.

Provide New Stretching Experiences

One of the ways to fight against micromanaging your associate staff is to invite them to try out new ministry roles and responsibilities. This is a proactive way of expressing your confidence in them and your expectation that they are capable of more than they have done in the past. While this again puts the staff member in the position of having to learn new things and take new risks, it demonstrates your trust in the staff member, and is an opportunity for new mentoring and coaching. Two of our associate staff members describe their experiences with this and how it boosts their confidence.

> *I think the thing I most appreciated there from my pastor was just a lot of trust. He trusted me, probably more than he should have, and gave me significant responsibilities. And the door was always open for me to come and ask, and say, "What am I supposed to do?" So that's probably the best thing that came out of his relationship with me. And I think that has transferred right over into what I do.*

> *A second thing that stands out is that he actually encouraged me to do unique things for outreach, and even to spend more money (I know this may sound strange). We were encouraged to try unique events, outreaches, fellowship activities, and were never discouraged in doing so because of finances. This made me feel as if I was trusted and recognized for good stewardship of the ministry's resources.*

Giving new responsibilities, and being available to help them learn how to successfully execute them, allows your staff members to grow on the job and helps you see them as capable, growing leaders. In turn, this can help you let go of micromanaging attitudes and behaviors.

Affirm Wherever Possible

One of the things we know about human nature is that we can often change our negative attitudes through a discipline of more positive thinking. An example of this is when we are feeling depressed, taking time to write out all of the blessings we have and are thankful for. Just reminding ourselves of these blessings lifts our spirits and allows us to see our situation in new ways. Paul understood something of this when he admonished the church in Philippi in his letter,

> *Finally, brothers, whatever is true, whatever is honorable, whatever is just, whatever is pure, whatever is lovely, whatever is commendable, if there is any excellence, if there is anything worthy of praise, think about these things.*
> (Philippians 4:8)

To fight against tendencies toward micromanaging, it may be helpful to take time to reflect on the gifts and abilities of your associate staff members, writing out what you are thankful for about them and their ministry, and to share that with them. It can help you refocus away from your fears of what may not go well and have a greater confidence in your staff that allows you to back off from "hovering" over them. If you find yourself hovering, asking too many detailed questions, or offering too much advice, it would be good to ask yourself why this might be, and if you are willing and able to take the risk of backing off a bit and allowing your staff member the space to demonstrate what they are capable of. You may find your fears and concerns decreasing and your associate staff member feeling more trusted.

In that spirit, let me close this section with a few quotes from some supervising pastors about the ways they try to create a supportive environment for their associate staff members to serve in and how they have adapted as their staff members have grown.

> *There's this philosophy where, you were invited to be on the staff because you are gifted and called to fill this position, and we believe in you. So we will allocate resources, we will prayerfully support, and there is accountability to that, but there's a lot of freedom for them to do their ministry.*

> *What I tell our staff is, "I hired you to be the professional. If I'm doing your job, then one of us is not needed. Stay in touch with me, keep me aware of what's going on. I'll drop in, see what you're doing, let's have lunch together." Drop in their office, see what's going on, but I'm not going to be a helicopter senior pastor hovering over every meeting.*

> *You see somebody grow as they're assimilating into the church culture, they're doing their job well. We have a lot of freedom for how we want to do what we're tasked to do. We don't tell the student ministers or kids ministers*

here's how you need to do your job. We say here's what we want, we want it to be a safe place for the kids to come and learn, where they can have fun, they can eventually have chances to receive Christ, where they can serve. You figure out whatever program you want to do, as long as you're accomplishing these goals.

That's a very, very delicate balance. Getting somebody to that place obviously takes time. It also takes a lot of energy because it's a choice to choose when to trust, and when to let go, and when to inquire and go in detail with them. So as you watch them, it's very much of an observing role, and it's being present. So when you're present and you watch how they handle something, and then what I always try to do is give feedback. . . .

. . . you stop going to every meeting that they're in charge of, because you trust that they're doing a good job. You've watched them. It's the, "I do, you watch, you do, I watch, you do, I go do something else," approach to oversight. And I tend to be a person who may move to that fairly quickly. But really because I'm fairly independent I'm sort of pushing people to be independent. "You can make this decision. You don't need to come to me with all these questions." For the most part you just kind of keep pushing it and trusting because you've seen some good patterns in that. And it's also giving increased responsibility.

TAKING INVENTORY

The focus of this chapter has been on practical ways to support the ministry efforts of your associate staff members, and avoid the trap of micromanagement. We've again provided some questions for your own reflection, and others for discussion with your staff members. We encourage you to consider finding a time with your staff to consider this together, allowing them to identify the questions they think may be most helpful to discuss together. As supervisors, our perspectives on how well things are going for our staff members can sometimes be overly optimistic, like looking through rose-colored glasses. It may be helpful to plan an extended time together for this conversation, allowing your associate staff to take the lead in reflection on what they see going well, and what may need attention.

Keeping Up without Hovering

Leader: Do you feel that you are keeping up with what is happening in the ministry areas your associate staff members lead? When was the last time you visited their ministry area to see what was happening and encourage those involved?

With Your Associates: Do you feel as though I adequately understand the challenges of your ministry areas? Would it be good for me to visit sometime? If so, what could I do there that would be helpful to you and those you work with?

Ensuring They Have the Needed Resources

Leader: Have your associate staff members struggled to get the resources they need for their ministries? Do you understand what their needs are? Are you in a position to help rally support and resources for them?

With Your Associates: Are you struggling at all to get the resources you need for your ministry area? If so, how might I be of help? What do you need, or what roadblocks might I be able to address that would make things easier for you?

Coordinating with Other Ministries

Leader: Do you see your staff members competing for resources (funding, facilities, personnel), or do they collaborate in support of one another's ministry areas? Do you have policies and procedures in place to help staff with coordinating their ministries?

With Your Associates: Do you feel as though you are competing with other associate staff members, or with me, for resources, like funds, use of facilities, or volunteer staff? What challenging experiences have you had recently? How might we better coordinate our ministries together?

Developing Congregational and Lay Leader Support

Leader: Are some of your associate staff members, and their ministry areas, not really visible to the congregation? How might you be an advocate for them and their ministry areas, raising the value and encouraging participation? Do your lay leaders understand the extent and importance of what the associate staff are doing in ministry? How can you help them better understand and support the work of the associate staff?

With Your Associates: Do you feel that the members of the congregation, and the lay leaders of the church, really understand and appreciate the importance of your ministry area? What would you like them to know and value about these ministry areas? What kind of support do you feel you need from them that you have not recently had?

Backing Them Up as Needed

Leader: How do you handle situations where criticism is brought to you about an associate staff member? What would be the appropriate steps to address this the next time a criticism is brought to you?

With Your Associates: When you have faced criticism or had conflict with someone in the church, did you feel that you were adequately supported? If not, what would you appreciate in the future if someone came to me (supervisor) with a complaint or concern?

Avoiding Micromanaging and Neglect

Leader: Are you purposefully seeking to adapt your supervision style to the growth of each of your associate staff members? Are there things you have done in the past that are no longer needed now that they have grown on the job? Are you giving staff members the freedom to fail, and helping them learn from those experiences? Are you looking for new stretching experiences for your staff that will encourage them to continue to grow and develop their gifts?

With Your Associates: Are there things I have done recently as a supervisor that either made you feel neglected or felt like too much "micromanaging" of your work? Where do you feel like you need more guidance? Where are you feeling more comfortable and no longer need as much guidance? Have you felt the freedom to pursue new ministry initiatives in your area? If not, what has made that hard for you? Do you feel as though you are ready to try out some new ministry responsibilities at the church? If so, what could you see yourself getting involved in?

Following Up: In light of what I have considered and/or we have discussed above, what needs to be given priority and addressed in the near future? What is important but can wait a while before we address it? When and where will these items be followed up on?

Chapter Six

Supporting Staff Personally

Mick Boersma

Fifteen years into my sojourn as a professor of pastoral ministry, I found myself enjoying lunch one day with my longtime mentor, Wally. For some months, I'd been considering the possibility of leaving the academic world and returning to the pastorate. A number of personal and professional factors were conspiring to cause some insecurities about my calling.

Since Wally had been my pastor during my high school and college years, he knew me well. We had even ministered together at a district level in our denomination. Our families were well acquainted. He had followed my career into the pastorate and academia. We were friends.

Over coffee and dessert, he listened, asked questions, and offered loving, honest, and godly counsel. His support that day gave me a renewed sense of my place in God's work, an appreciation for the amazing privilege I was enjoying, and a settled peace to continue forward into new opportunities of service as a teacher.

Our encounter that day represents the incredible power and benefit that accrues when a ministry supervisor supports his or her staff in a deeply personal way. Kevin and I found in our research that, apart from support in the day-to-day ministry context (see chapter 5), effective supervision of staff members must include more intimate personal support.

This kind of support can include myriad possibilities. Yet, among responses from supervisors and staff, three key areas are repeatedly mentioned as most appreciated.

WHERE YOUR STAFF WELCOMES PERSONAL SUPPORT

Their Spiritual Life

It is not uncommon for supervising pastors to assume the staff is spiritually mature. After all, they are leaders in the congregation, right? But the reality is often quite different. Aside from the usual challenge of growing deeper into the faith, any staff member can struggle at various times in life for myriad reasons. Effective supervisors are not only aware of this possibility, but they also work to encourage and resource their colleagues on the journey. One lead pastor candidly shares his perspective on this oft-neglected area of concern:

> *I think we've been so obsessed with leadership and vision and church growth in the last generation that we kind of assume everyone's doing okay in their own spiritual walk and development, and we focus on leadership and competency and skill. I'm certainly not against all that, but I think of that in tandem with helping people develop spiritually. I think where I hear a supervisor is doing a great job, there's again an authentic interest in that and time given to it.*

Another supervising pastor underscores the crucial significance of encouraging the spiritual life of associate staff:

> *If we abide in Christ, we'll bear fruit. Apart from him we can do nothing. So we say our first job as ministers is to abide in Christ and stay connected. The expectation is we will maintain a strong connected devotional walk with Christ, trusting that as he's growing us, we'll grow people. This is a marathon, not a sprint, we want you for the long haul, and please, we have to take care of our souls. Leadership is living a life worthy of imitation, and we're modeling for our team leaders, our life group leaders, for our church family, what it means to live a highly committed life for the long haul. And so, that's our first value. Soul-filled service, and there's a high emphasis on maintaining our walk with God.*

Wally always used to counsel me, "You will only lead your people spiritually as far as you are willing to go yourself." Thriving as a supervisor means a growing walk with the Lord, and a willingness to help your colleagues journey with you toward spiritual maturity.

Their Family Life

Whether married or single, our respondents highlighted the significance of family support from their supervisors. The following pastors share their appreciation for such care:

The supervising pastor pursued a personal relationship with me and my family. We became friends even more than partners in ministry. It was healthy and enjoyable. We could talk about sin and struggles.

He always asks about my family . . . [his] following up on what I've shared helps me to feel connected even though he may not be directly involved in my ministry.

It helped to relieve stress when we could talk family and acknowledge that our families are supposed to be our first ministry. It made me feel like a member of a church, not just a cog on the wheel of the ministry machine.

Pastoral families face unique challenges, of course. One longtime senior pastor provides a heartening look into the nature of his support for his younger staff:

. . . I'm older. This is a huge advantage. And our kids have all done well. So that is super helpful. At the same time, we're still parenting, so I'm convinced anybody who wrote a parenting book just quit having kids. So there's still a sense of "oh no, what do we do now?" I think we're a safe place for them, to say "our kids are . . . this is what's going on, or I caught them on the Internet doing this. . . ."

What a blessing to know that your family is highly valued by those in authority over you—that they understand the challenges of ministry families!

Their Professional (Career) Life

The third major area of personal support mentioned focuses on one's personal professional development and career path. While a part of supporting a staff person's ministry (chapter 5), this support focuses on the individual's calling and career path. In one case, a supervising pastor mentions how a senior staff person provided guidance leading to their present career:

I think in my very early days in ministry, I was never going to go into children's ministries. It was not my desire, or my goal in life to be a full-time minister. That just never crossed my mind, but to have a supervisor look at me and say, "You have such gifts in this, but is this something you really want to do, or can you see yourself doing something else?" To care for me in that process, to care for me and who am I? What are you made of, what experiences have you had in life to get you to this point? What are the leadership skills that they saw in me, or the personal gifts that they saw in me, and how those things would contribute to a future in ministry, was very touching.

As we polled and interviewed supervising pastors, nearly all of them indicated they had previous experience as staff members under another's supervision. Unsurprisingly, most were very appreciative of the career coaching and skill development they received from their supervisors.

Before we turn our attention to specific approaches taken by effective supervising pastors in supporting their staff, it is paramount to understand the environment needed for success. Our findings indicate a very clear picture of what is required for genuine and fruitful personal support of one's staff.

A HEALTHY ENVIRONMENT FOR PERSONAL SUPPORT

My mentor's wise and loving guidance that day over lunch was a true blessing. But it was not received in a vacuum. Throughout the years, an environment was established that facilitated the effective support he shared that day. Indeed, my experience reflects what one pastor saw in his own:

> We met regularly to talk about ministry activities and personal growth. His presence was warm, understanding, and accepting.

Based on feedback from our respondents, two key elements must be pursued in order to create a supportive environment for personal spiritual growth, family health, and professional career development.

Relationship

If any one theme dominates the story line of powerful ministry, it is the importance of healthy relationships. Effective ministers engage in building kinship with those they supervise. The depth of those connections is not as important, we find, as the assurance staff have of a sincere desire to know them personally. One seasoned senior pastor shares a biblical reflection regarding his experience as a supervisor of a multiple-staff church:

> A Scripture that has been a little bit of an anchor for me in supervision is John 15:14, where Jesus says, "You are my friend if you do what I command. I no longer call you servants, because a servant does not know his master's business. Instead I've called you friend. Everything I've learned from my father I've made known to you." So I've taken that as something of a model, recognizing that you can't just be best buddies and do everything together, but a friendship relationship with my staff, in trying to lay bare my soul and have an open honest relationship as friends would. Try to let them know where I'm at in my own spiritual journey. . . .

Another comments on how the pursuit of relationship has enabled his elders to support the staff, as well:

I see them [lay leaders] praying for our care pastor, and reaching out to him. And that's because it's a mutual relationship there that as our staff cares for them, they naturally reciprocate that care. There's not necessarily a program, I think when you have good healthy relationships, those things just naturally flow out of that.

While relationship building does occur in staff meetings (see chapter 3), often this is all the personal attention a staff person receives. That's not enough for thriving, according to many of the supervising pastors we interviewed. One highly experienced lead pastor (an octogenarian) shared this frustration heard from many associate staff members he's known over the years:

I think the biggest one I've heard from staff about their pastor is that the pastor doesn't meet with us, or he has his business meeting and it's over. And I encourage pastors, even though you're meeting with your staff almost weekly, make sure that you meet with them individually at least every couple weeks, "how're you doing George, what's happening?" You've got to build that personal relationship. You've got to do it.

How supervisors manage to build relationships can take many forms. One pastor's approach seems to encapsulate the variety:

I wouldn't say that the staff members, that we're all best friends, because we have a lot of ministry to do, but we do share life together. Some of us golf together. . . . It's kind of neat right now, there's a group of about four or five of our staff members that probably three times a week, they'll go down and have lunch together. Some of them are walking together, and they'll take a walk around the lake. There's a lot of life sharing.

"Life sharing." While not always easy or natural, building a growing, honest, intentional relationship with your associate staff is essential. It does not have to be complicated, but just showing an interest in their lives and being together outside the professional ministry bubble. We find that work colleagues just want to be known and appreciated for who they are.

Safety

There is no fear in love, but perfect love casts out fear. For fear has to do with punishment, and whoever fears has not been perfected in love. (1 John 4:18)

There is a lot of anxiety out there on ministry teams. We hear regularly of staff being forced to leave or fired outright. Caring for a colleague at the deeper personal level will not happen if they sense danger in sharing their struggles. One lead pastor relates this tale involving a former supervising pastor:

> *He didn't foster an environment of transparency among the pastors. There was this sense that, "You'd better have your stuff together or else I will remove you." This, in turn, caused me to put up a facade and not be open with others when times were tough spiritually. I didn't ask for help when I needed it because there was a culture of "pastors should be super-men." When my wife and I were having difficulties that I finally divulged, they didn't walk me through that time. I was indefinitely "benched" and became a janitor. Only after the fall-out did the Administrative pastor offer to meet with me if I wanted. However, I didn't feel close enough to him to open up about anything. It would have been better if one of my supervising pastors had already established an ongoing relationship with me . . . gotten coffee with me once a month or something.*

Here we see that pursuit of a relationship was missing, which very likely would have helped establish a greater sense of security. As another pastor succinctly puts it:

> *You only get authenticity if it's safe to be authentic. So then, in that context people can grow.*

Establishing a safe place within your relationship to staff is critical for thriving. To create this as a supervisor, you must be confident and secure in who you are—both in Christ, and in your calling. Supervisors who are easily threatened by the authenticity of a staff member will not be able to provide that sanctuary in which healing can be realized. Would that all ministry leaders reflected this happy situation:

> *My head pastor allowed me to be in process, imperfect. I know his prayers were with me as I worked through my own issues, but his words were uncondemning and supportive.*

It must be said here that even within a safe environment, it is often difficult for staff to share deep personal issues with their supervisors. Knowledge changes things, and sharing certain areas of struggle may be too impactful to the daily work relationship. In such cases, having someone to turn to, as I did with my mentor Wally, can provide the setting for healing and growth. Many ministries are available today to which pastors can turn for personal encouragement and resources. Some of these are listed in our "Resources for Supervising Pastors" in appendix A. Yet, happy is the one who can find solid help closer to home, even from his or her ministry colleagues.

APPROACHES TO PROVIDING PERSONAL SUPPORT

As Kevin and I have listened to supervising pastors, former staff pastors, and the hundreds of ministry students and alumni we've networked with throughout our ministry careers, several approaches to personal support have been identified. While it would be tempting to suggest that encouraging your staff personally is complicated or out of reach for most mortals, such need not be the case.

Everything we've seen and heard points to three basic ways staff really "feel the love." They are prayer, personal counsel, and what we'll call "deeds of love." Essentially, supporting staff is all about being a shepherd to them, leading, guiding, teaching, caring, protecting. As one senior pastor comments:

> *Most of it is, I would say, just trying to shepherd them. Stay connected about what's going on with their kids, marriages. And because my wife and I have been at this longer than they have, we have a lot to offer there. Praying with them, we do some social things together. Probably not enough, because it just feels like everybody's always busy. Most of it's just natural shepherding. I just make them the priority of my shepherding, and so does my wife.*

Prayer

Ministry is challenging work. It's busy and there's lots to do—all the time. The temptation to focus on supervising all the activity can cause a leader to overlook supporting his or her coworkers at a deep, personal level. And one of the most powerful avenues for providing such support is prayer.

> Therefore, confess your sins to one another and pray for one another, that you may be healed. The prayer of a righteous person has great power as it is working. (James 5:16)

> *I love the times of personal prayer with the pastor.*

Few actions endear us to others more than when we pray for them. It is one of the great privileges of being a child of God—to enter God's presence through prayer. Whether confession is involved or not, lifting others up in sincere prayer is one of the most powerful ministries believers can share. Supervising pastors who pray for and with their staff make this privilege a key part of their support. In the areas of their personal, family, and professional life, staff appreciate the following approach to prayer (table 6.1):

Be purposeful—Often prayer is relegated to times of challenge when we need God's wisdom, protection, or guidance. While God is ready to hear and help, it's far better to keep prayer a regular part of our personal spiritual

Table 6.1.   Praying For and With Your Associate Staff

Be purposeful

Be attentive

Be vulnerable

Be trustworthy

Be wholesome

routine. And so should it be in our pastoral team settings. Even in the context of regular staff meetings (see chapters 3 and 4), deeper, more personal prayer ministry can be realized:

> *Well, we always have a time of prayer at our weekly staff meetings. . . . Sometimes we'll pair up and we'll pray for each other, sometimes share prayer requests.*

> *We have a staff meeting every Monday, that basically goes from 11 to 2:30, and when we meet at 11 o'clock it's for pastoral staff and families, prayer support. And we literally just come into our conference room, sit down and say, how are you guys doing, and who can we pray for? It becomes a very transparent, active, honest time of saying things like "hey I'm looking for a new car" or "my mom's being admitted to a care home for dementia" or "I got a doctor's appointment" or "I've got a real difficult person in my ministry."*

Be attentive—Sometimes our ministry colleagues are struggling, needing someone to pray for them, but may be too shy, ashamed, or preoccupied in the midst of their crisis to ask. Our staff colleagues usually appreciate the interest and concern demonstrated when others ask them how things are going—and find a listening ear:

> *I appreciate the encouragement and support emotionally and spiritually by taking time to ask and pray about my personal life beyond ministry concerns.*

> *Somehow I'm able to read people's spirits pretty well, and when I sense discouragement or inattentiveness in a staff meeting, I try to follow that up, and connect. Do a Starbucks run, or lunch or something with the person, and find out how I can be supportive, or what is it. What was troubling you today?*

Be vulnerable—People open up when we do the same. When the environment is safe, and the participants are honest, effective prayer can accomplish much, indeed. The context can be in staff meetings or in more private settings:

My head pastor's transparency and vulnerability allowed us to share an open relationship and lean on the Lord together for the healing we both needed.

Be trustworthy—Again, safety is required. Trust is something of great value, and nearly impossible to recover once violated. What is shared in personal and corporate prayer settings must stay in the room. Not all associates enjoy such confidence:

Perhaps one of the biggest areas that I felt unsupported was in my personal life. I was married four months prior to assuming the assistant pastor role, and I found the environment for pastors and their spouses to be one that was not safe to discuss personal matters and to really pray for one another. I went outside the church to find this for myself, relying on two friends who were pastors elsewhere, but this was especially hard for my wife. She struggled to find others who were safe to talk to about ministry frustrations.

Be wholesome—As mentioned above, we often resort to prayer when things are tough. Personal prayer support for staff can become a sort of "triage" response to the rigors and disappointments of pastoral ministry. As team leaders, it is important to keep prayer wholesome, inclusive of adoration, confession, thanksgiving, and petition.

Back at the restaurant, Wally led me through my personal angst to a celebration of God's goodness. His prayer was one of thanksgiving, appreciation, and hope for his protégé's present and future life of ministry.

Personal Counsel

Everyone can use a little therapy once in awhile. Whether that comes through informal conversation or professional appointment, we need a little "assist" at times to work through problems, dilemmas, or difficult decisions. Few pastoral staff can afford licensed counselor care, should they need it. Some congregations offer such assistance to their staff, but most go wanting in their time of need. Our findings show that to the degree possible, effective supervising pastors provide personal counsel to their staff at their various levels of need. And it is appreciated:

For personal problems, I always felt comfortable going to them [supervisors]. I remember after I got married, I was on the phone with my pastor for a few hours trying to solve a problem I had with my husband. My pastor was there for me and helped us through that time.

Providing competent counsel to staff is also a frustration to many. Lack of training, time, and experience causes one lead pastor to lament:

Just recently I have been so much thinking about further deeper development for those that I lead, meaning coaching, counseling. Some of them deeply need counseling for past hurts. Family concerns, marriage issues, chronically ill kids. Counseling is so great, and I've been through it in my own life for different seasons and reasons. I don't have the capacity for that, and they need that.

Thankfully, more and more church and para church ministries are waking up to the need to provide individual and family counseling to their staff members. At the very least, such care is a wise investment. The cost of losing staff is far greater than most people can imagine. Highly skilled and costly to train, they are like fighter pilots. The air force will go to all lengths to find a downed aviator. Their life is precious, of course. But so is the reservoir of knowledge and experience they possess. This pastor's former supervisor obviously understood the strategic value of personal counsel for his staff, in the context of both work and personal issues:

He made space for me within his own schedule. We met regularly to talk about ministry activities and personal growth. His presence was warm, understanding, & accepting. He drew from his own experiences, both positive & negative, in providing counsel and support. This helped me to overcome my own challenges with less fear, knowing that those who've gone before me also dealt with similar obstacles in their paths.

Counsel can take many forms. Conferences can provide a more anonymous and less threatening context for pastoral staff to work on their life and ministry issues. Retreats offer a bit more focused approach. Personal meetings with a trained professional are often more anxiety producing, but can lead to more significant progress. But most church staff will experience the "let's sit down over coffee" scenario involving a good friend or supportive ministry colleague. In the context of a healthy and safe relationship, both supervisor and his or her staff can gain much.

Deeds of Love

As the apostle Paul languished in a Roman prison, he penned a letter to the believers in Philippi. A church that gave him great joy, he was particularly grateful for the financial aid they had sent along, and the company of their beloved brother Epaphroditus. Their deeds of love gave rise to his words,

I thank my God in all my remembrance of you . . . because of your partnership in the gospel from the first day until now. (Philippians 1:3, 5)

Their love was more than words. Money was sent. A dear and treasured brother embarked on a dangerous journey to be physically present with Paul.

This kind of tangible care is what our surveys and interviews highlighted over and over again. The examples could be nearly infinite, but we will focus on acts of kindness evidenced in those three key areas where associate staff appreciate support.

In Their Spiritual Life

Unfortunately, we often hear of situations in which the business of ministry crowds out any purposeful attention to the soul care of staff. Happily, several of our supervising pastors mentioned the priority given to spiritual development during regular staff meetings. Here's a sampling:

> *We really try to have this culture where we don't just see you as a person who's here to help us accomplish the vision of the church, we care about you and want you to grow.*

> *Every Wednesday from ten to noon, we have our weekly staff meeting. How that staff meeting's structured is the first half hour is given to some type of devotional and prayer time together. So it's almost like a cell-group, family group, life group. And the reason for that is, I feel like our staff members are always pouring out to others, it's kind of a time where I feel like I need to pour into them. So we do devotions together, and then we pray for one another, and that's the first thing on the agenda.*

> *Usually we stop a couple times during the staff meeting to pray for some things specific to the church, or if somebody's facing some real challenges on the staff. Sometimes we'll pair up and we'll pray for each other, sometimes share prayer requests.*

Another senior pastor of a large church plans regular prayer retreats with his staff:

> *One of the things I try to schedule quarterly is to take the staff away from the campus for, I call it a half-day of prayer. And I've tried to teach them and give them some formats for how to spend some time in personal worship, reflection, anticipation, cleansing, asking God, "Search me oh God, know my heart."*

Providing time and funds for staff members to connect with a spiritual director is more available now than in years past. Such services are often a part of denominational support, and there are independent ministries around the world with this focus. Personal retreats, conferences, and sabbaticals designed for spiritual growth are valuable approaches to consider, as well.

In Their Family Life

We recognize that not all staff are married, but everyone is part of a family, and needs in this part of our life are numerous and ongoing. The supervising pastors we talked to mentioned ways they are being supported and also providing encouragement to their own staff:

> *I think about the staff, their personal lives, their spouses, their financial concerns, their children, their business, their schedule. I interact with them daily about these matters. Caring for elderly parents.*

Our long-term research has shown that supervising pastors are in a unique place to encourage fair compensation and benefits for their staff. It is awkward, and often seen as inappropriate, for staff to "wave their own flag" in this regard. This support can come by championing raises and benefits to the senior pastor or church board. In one case, a lead pastor's kindness led this staff member to share:

> *One time I was struggling to pay the bills and I sat with my pastor and planned for that conversation to be about me quitting. But my pastor, even before I could give him my resignation, gave me an envelope of $500 and said, "I know you've been struggling and this is just a little something to help you get you by." That day, after he gave me that money, I realized how much he cared for me and it really made an impact and made me stick it through and I'm glad I did.*

Several of our conversations related to simple acts of kindness shown to staff, by both paid and volunteer ministry leaders:

> *Taking care of the family. I think a few staff members; they have disabled children. So sometimes helping with money. Or visiting their families.*

> *We see, especially in most of the ministry areas, the lay leadership really take care of those ministry leaders. I was just thinking for example—the youth pastor had a baby a little while ago. His youth mentors are the ones that rallied around and arranged meals, did the shower, all that stuff. We have in our care ministry different leaders over divorce care, grief care.*

> *I keep my ears open for things going on, so if I know that one of my guys, their wife's home sick, I'll send him home. Hey, do you really have to be here today? Go home at one, go home after lunch, take care of the wife, take care of the family. Just really help them to care for their families when there's crises going on.*

Research has shown in recent years that most American workers do not take their entire vacation allowances. They may love their work, or be afraid they'll lose their jobs. Whatever the case, the value of getting some time away is lost, and the benefits along with it. Pastoral staff often follow this pattern, but a supportive supervisor will protect and encourage the use of vacation time, as well as seek to provide sabbatical leave. One such supporting lead pastor relates:

> *We don't want your family to hate the church, we don't want your kids to grow up and say gosh we're scarred because my dad was a pastor, he was never home. We really try to look out for each other in that sense. We have built in every seventh year, now sometimes it might not be until the 8th or 9th, but if possible we try to give each staff member a sabbatical.*

In addition to such basic expressions of love and care, associate staff can benefit from marriage and family counseling. National organizations exist for this purpose, and many regional ministries have been created to uphold pastoral families. Supervisors who encourage and procure such resources for their staff not only show love but also wisdom:

> *It's been a huge part of my heart to support the staff and their well-being, because their well-being directly impacts the work of the ministry. I mean if things are rough in their marriage, there are things that come out in the work environment. Attitudes, actions, behaviors, that are very noticeable.*

In Their Professional (Career) Life

Supporting the staff in professional growth in their ministry area will be addressed in chapter 7. Our focus here is on the broader view of personal career development, assisting your team members in navigating their life calling. In pursuit of this, you should consider securing expense accounts through which your staff members can take seminary courses, attend conferences, secure published resources, and maybe join a professional guild that will facilitate long-range professional growth. However, a supervising pastor can provide assistance to their colleagues in-house, too.

During my pastorate in the Pacific Northwest, several individuals and married couples (including one on our staff) expressed a desire to prepare for senior pastoral or missions service. In cooperation with our deacon board, and with the support of the congregation, my wife and I brought them alongside us and trained them. Many of these families have been serving in pastorates and para church ministries since then. We spent hours together exploring the responsibilities of shepherding people and gave them ample opportunity to exercise and develop their pastoral skills and philosophy of ministry. This reflects what one pastor experienced under his supervising pastor:

> *He asked about my future ministry goals and included experiences and feedback to grow towards. He also gave regular opportunities to preach at the*

midweek Bible study. These areas were helpful because I learned how to grow people not just the program.

Sharing the work of ministry and enabling your staff to explore and realize their own dreams is an act of love. After all, as was our experience, you may lose them from the team as they pursue that future. As Kevin and I talked with and read responses from supervising pastors, it became apparent that others had invested in all of them—those who, whether consciously or not, had prepared them for the next step in their career of service. We all stand on the shoulders of those who have gone before. For me, that includes Wally. I will never forget that lunch conversation. The last fifteen years have been a blessing, in part because of his wise, honest, and loving counsel.

TAKING INVENTORY

Like our last chapter, this one covers a wide range of issues. As supervisors, we sometimes do not adequately understand or appreciate the challenges our associate staff members are facing, and what they would value as personal support. It would be good to find times to review the different topics we've addressed, either in one extended conversation or over several times of meeting together, and determine which ones need some reflection and discussion. Some topics may be appropriate for a group discussion, while others may benefit from some one-on-one conversation. We hope these will be helpful to you and your associates.

Building a Healthy Environment for Personal Support

Relationship

Leader: How available am I to my associate staff? In what ways can I communicate my desire to be available to them when needed, but also protect the time I need to fulfill my own ministry responsibilities?

With Your Associates: Am I clearly communicating my schedule to you on a regular basis? Are there ways I signal a lack of desire to be available to you? How might I make my availability more obvious and inviting?

Leader: Do I have a sense of how approachable I am as a person? How do I deal with criticism or complaints from others (including my staff)?

With Your Associates: Do I give the impression I am not interested in building a relationship with you? If so, how do I communicate that disinterest? What can I do to convey a more open posture toward our relationship? Are there ways I react to criticism that are unhelpful for our relationship?

Leader: Am I comfortable with the idea that my associate staff members look to me to be an example to them in spiritual growth, ministry integrity, and openness to learn? Is there anything that I fear will cause them to lose respect for me as their leader? What steps can I take to address these concerns?

With Your Associates: Are there areas of my leadership or life example that are less than helpful in your own spiritual and ministry development? Have I lost some of your respect due to an incident or attitude in the past or present? Could you share that and give me an opportunity to make changes that will bring healing and growth to our relationship?

Safety

Leader: As I think over the last few months, have I been doing anything that might be hindering my associates' ability to trust me as their supervisor? What steps could I take to restore that trust?

With Your Associates: Do you feel safe as a member of this staff? If so, what brings you that sense of security? Do you feel unsafe as member of this staff? Could you share why you are feeling insecure as a part of the team? What could I do to bring about a safer environment among us?

Leader: Is there anything I can do to communicate better my desire to have my associates share freely with me their ideas, concerns, and frustrations?

With Your Associates: Do you feel comfortable sharing your ideas, concerns, and frustrations with me? Have I responded in the past in ways that have discouraged you from openly sharing these things? What might I do to encourage you to share your heart and mind going forward?

Leader: What level of transparency characterizes how my associates and I talk with each other? Would our ability to work together be enhanced by greater authenticity than we currently have? How might I begin moving in that direction?

With Your Associates: Do you sense that you know the "real" me, or does it feel to you as if I'm being artificial in our personal and/or working relationship? If transparency is not present, how could we work together to make that a significant aspect of our relationship? Would you feel safe exploring this concern? If not, what would make you hesitate?

Approaches to Providing Personal Support

Prayer

Leader: Do I regularly pray for and with my associate staff members? Do I pray for both their ministry and their personal needs? Do I let them know that I am praying for them?

With Your Associates: Do we have enough set times during which we can pray together? What schedule would be helpful for you—time of day, day of the week, duration? How can I best be apprised of your prayer needs on a regular basis?

Leader: Do I encourage others in our ministry to pray for and with my associate staff members?

With Your Associates: How could we set up accountability in this endeavor? Is there a mechanism that could facilitate awareness of one another's prayer items (alerts, e-mails)?

Leader: Are there ways I could help my staff identify prayer partners, given their areas of ministry and gender?

With Your Associates: What conditions would make you comfortable partnering with another staff member for the purpose of prayer? Why might you hesitate to team up with someone in this regard?

Personal Counsel

Leader: Do I find myself focused primarily with how well my associates' ministries are going, and not paying much attention to how they are doing personally?

With Your Associates: Do you feel heard when you come and share concerns or ministry situations with me? Do I seem to care more about your performance than about you as a colleague and fellow servant in Christ? What could I do to change this perception?

Leader: Am I providing a safe environment that frees my staff to honestly approach their personal areas of struggle? What can I do to create such freedom?

With Your Associates: Do you feel safe to share your struggles with me or others on our staff? If so, what makes it easy for you to do so? If not, why is it difficult to open up with your concerns? What would a safe environment look like among our staff?

Leader: Am I vulnerable enough about my own "issues" so as to not be uncomfortable or threatened by my associates' disclosures?

With Your Associates: Do you find me hesitant to enter into conversation about certain subject areas? Would you characterize me as vulnerable? If not, how does this come across to you in our interactions? What areas of concern might I be more open about concerning my own life?

Leader: Does our church facilitate confidential professional counseling services for our staff and encourage them to take advantage of such help when needed?

With Your Associates: As your supervisor, what could I do to encourage you to take advantage of professional counseling as needed? Does our church offer sufficient referral service and financial aid to you? Are we maintaining an environment around here that conveys an affirming approach to seeking counsel for personal and professional needs?

Deeds of Love

Leader: Am I aware of the particular challenges each of my staff members is facing in their personal and ministry life? What can I do to become more enlightened?

With Your Associates: What could I do to provide an opportunity for you to share your personal and ministry challenges? Could we plan a regular schedule for attending to these items through discussion and prayer? How can I provide concrete assistance in your most pressing areas of need at this time?

Leader: Is there flexibility in my associates' schedules to allow them to have time with their families, especially when evening and weekend demands are heavy?

With Your Associates: What particular pressures are you currently experiencing in terms of time with your family and/or loved ones? What would be your ideal schedule for time off during the typical workweek? Are there times of the year that call for changes in your time off? How can I facilitate you enjoying flexibility for such periods?

Leader: Am I an advocate to the church governing board to provide a fair salary and benefit package to my associate staff?

With Your Associates: How could I be a helpful advocate for you with the governing board of the church regarding salary and benefits? Do you think the current procedure for determining salaries and benefits is effective? If not, how could I advocate for constructive changes? What are your particular concerns right now regarding salary and benefits?

Leader: Do I encourage my associates to take regular advantage of continuing education opportunities, to participate in professional organizations, and to benefit from personal spiritual growth opportunities?

With Your Associates: Am I providing enough guidance and networking to assist you in discovering avenues of educational and professional advancement in your field of ministry? Are there ways in which I can help provide you with personal spiritual growth opportunities? Have I supported you adequately before the governing board in these areas of growth and development?

Leader: Does my church or ministry provide staff with time and money to do the kinds of things listed in the item above? If not, what steps could I take to encourage the leadership to do more in this area?

With Your Associates: Do you feel the current budget allocation for continuing education in your area of ministry is sufficient? If not, where are needs going unmet, and how much would be appropriate? Is the present time off given to pursue professional guilds and more education sufficient for your needs at this time?

Chapter Seven

Staff Review and Development

Mick Boersma

The title of this chapter may evoke a smile or dredge up painful memories—or both. For one of my former church deacons, a seasoned senior pastor who had transitioned to service as a chaplain, his annual performance review sent him to the medicine cabinet for nerve pills. It seemed as if every year, at the annual congregational meeting, the parishioners would discuss their pastor's overall performance, with him in the room. The yearly inquisition left him bitter, by his own admission, and factored into his leaving parish ministry altogether.

Conversely, there is the experience of a newly graduated seminarian I met early in my tenure here. He was single, with little field experience, yet was desiring a preaching position in a local church. Having accepted my counsel regarding the realities of life, he secured a youth pastorate locally where he was taken under wing by a gracious and effective senior pastor. There he was trained, given increasing opportunity, and reviewed charitably on a regular basis and married the church chairman's daughter. He and his bride continue to serve faithfully and effectively over thirty years later.

Such is the importance, the impact, of staff review and development. The supervising pastors we have interviewed and polled, almost all of whom have been associates under former lead pastors, would counsel the following concerning staff reviews and development (table 7.1).

STAFF REVIEWS

Must Be Done—In a recent phone conversation with a young pastoral leader, he mentioned to me that the senior staff of his church was essentially "unaccountable" and distant from the larger staff. This was at a seemingly

Table 7.1.   Eleven Aspects of Profitable Staff Reviews

Reviews Must Be:	Done	Personalized
	Regular	Safe
	Documented	Honest
	Built on Clarity	Liberating
	Constructive	Developmental
	Culturally Informed	

"successful" church in a thriving urban setting. His comments reflect what another pastor shares:

> In the two mega churches I worked in there was either no annual review process or it was poorly done. I always felt blindsided by negative input. Relationships broke down and communication became almost non-existent. I felt isolated and unsupported.

A common theme in our research finds that staff reviews are infrequent, and if done at all, often mishandled. Reasons include what one pastor shares:

> The biggest factor that hindered my ability to perform my duties well was the fact that my job was not treated as a "job" but as a ministry (which I understand is true as all our roles are done unto Him). As a result, I was given no goals, regular evaluations, regular assessments . . . etc. which made it difficult to grow within the position.

This tendency to over-spiritualize the supervisor-staff relationship can shut down any meaningful and purposeful accountability that could lead to greater effectiveness and professional growth. The thought is: "We don't assess one another because we're not a business, but a ministry."

Another reason staff reviews may not happen is shared by this pastor serving in a cultural context where perceived success insulates staff members from accountability:

> Sometimes I think, if you have somebody that seems to be "successful," doing well in ministry, you're praised, adored, and left alone. And I think for young ministers that's one of the worst things that can happen to them. Because you develop all these awful bad habits, and your personal maturity is not in line with your professional strength. I saw that a lot in others and myself, and that makes it really hard when there's any sort of criticism.

One other rationale for shirking the staff review process is confessed by a supervising pastor whose colleagues have wanted more from him:

What I have heard from them over the years is, "We want more input from you. We want you to be telling us more things." More directive. I just wait upon them to come and say what am I supposed to do, or whatever? I mean if I see something, that's one thing, but I don't tend to micromanage at all. They feel like sometimes it's a lack of interest on my part, but it's really just a trust I have in them.

In this case, the team is working well, and the supervising pastor is content to let the machinery run without a lot of maintenance. I grew up on a farm, and one thing successful farmers always do is keep their equipment in top shape. Likewise, thriving ministry teams are led by supervisors who pay attention to the work and take the initiative in providing assessment and guidance.

Must Be Regular—You most likely have heard these words: "We need to talk." Whether coming from a spouse or work supervisor, most of us respond by breaking into a cold sweat. When staff reviews are rare, they often result in apprehension when they do occur. Our respondents consistently report that ongoing, regular accountability among colleagues is essential in keeping them effective as staff members:

My pastor kept me accountable. Not by micromanaging, but by regularly meeting with me and discussing my projects very openly.

We met up regularly to talk about ministry ideas and plans. He would follow up with our conversation and keep me accountable.

When I've gone through goals with the lead pastor and we regularly check in on them together, I feel supported and encouraged.

While annual reviews are typical, more regularity is preferred by many of those we interviewed. There is no magic frequency of such meetings, but more is better, according to this leader:

I'm also a fan of reviews, but not the kind of just formal annual review . . . that's the only time we check in. I often describe it as feeling like an IRS audit. That's not fun for anybody. So I really like a quarterly conversation that gets to where are you winning, what are some things that need to be shored up, how can I get you what you need? Early on in my ministry, by the time I needed to have a really hard conversation with a staff member, it was already a full-blown crisis. If I had done a better job of engaging problems early on we could have averted some of it, or it would have at least given my colleague more notice that there was a problem. I think having some kind of quarterly conversation that assesses how my staff is doing is a much better approach than a big formal annual review.

Some pastors mention their practice of debriefing immediately after major events, the reaching of major milestones, or even after the delivery of Sunday's sermon. Holding reviews while the memory is fresh can generate more factual and helpful conversation, correction, and planning for future team ministry. Chapters 3 and 4 have more to say about these practices.

Must Be Documented—One of my mentors once quipped, "If it isn't on paper, it doesn't exist." We can include digital files most certainly, but his point was helpful to me in my own supervising responsibilities. Staff reviews are challenging enough without the inaccuracies and misrepresentations that accompany verbal-only exchanges. Several of our effective supervising pastors note their practice of having staff members submit written reports to be reviewed before the face-to-face meeting. One reflects on how his supervisor provides preparatory questions for the staff review:

> *I had all the questions, and I had filled them all out and then sent them to him, and then we met for the review. And some of the items were . . . what was your worst day this year, what was your best day, why? What is your favorite thing about your ministry, what is your least favorite, where do you want to grow?*

Writing things down is often not a natural habit of pastors. One frankly admits:

> *Supervision is honestly the part that I've kind of had to kick into gear recently, because it's a discipline. Having a bi-weekly meeting with direct reports is necessary for me because every other week we have that accountability, where they're going to come and bring their ministry projects and questions, but then I'm going to refer back to what we've talked about in previous meetings. I take notes, not detailed notes, but just generic enough that I know we talked about this issue, or this volunteer, or this situation. What's the follow up on that? How's it going with that? That's been a discipline for me.*

The benefits of written interaction are worth the time and energy expended. As you'll see mentioned in chapter 8, they can assist not only in maintaining a clear understanding between supervisor and staff member but also provide guidance for corrective measures when necessary.

Must Be Built on Clarity—Speaking of "corrective measures," staff reviews are beneficial for purposes of guidance, course change, and other adjustments that will enhance a staff member's ministry effectiveness and personal growth. In order to be so, clear expectations, job descriptions, and goals are essential. It is difficult, if not impossible, to review a person's ministry if the basic parameters are not in place or understood between supervisor and staff. Comments from our research group include:

> *I've developed a bit more of a formal review process with the team, setting expectations for the year, goals, measurable things, and then following up with them throughout the year.*

One of the things that we didn't really do well . . . and maybe this falls under expectations . . . to have really good job descriptions. Having very good expectations about this is what you're responsible for, this is what we're measuring you by when you bring people on board. That's something we've learned over the years.

I think if I could change one thing, I would hold people a little bit more accountable in a more specific way. So that they would know that I have some expectations, and we could monitor whether they're meeting those or not. I think there's something healthy about that.

Clarity comes when job descriptions, expectations, goals, and assessments are written down and agreed upon. Without good definition, staff reviews can become exercises in futility where personal feelings are hurt and misunderstandings abound. Effective supervisors shield their staff from such disablement.

Must Be Constructive—Unlike the inquisition my former deacon experienced while in his pastorate, staff reviews ought to be uplifting and enriching in nature. There should be robust discussion between colleagues, give and take, a wholesome exchange of ideas and assessments, all in the context of careful listening. Far from being punitive, staff reviews are opportunities to strengthen staff members in their areas of service. Two supervising pastors share their upbeat approach:

We have a big culture of accountability, speaking in truth and love, and giving constructive feedback. That starts with me. We do a Saturday night service and then our Sunday morning service. And after every Saturday night service I sit down with all the pastors and we critique the message. What needs to happen here, what changes, any errors? Because we have a chance to make this better for tomorrow, so we're going to take the opportunity to do that. And me being open and vulnerable to critique in that situation just sets the tone for the whole staff. That no one's above loving instructive criticism and critique.

I've tried to annually give to the staff, in January, an evaluation where they can just let me know what gives them their greatest joy in their present ministry. What in the past year do you look back on with accomplishment? What would you like to accomplish next year? What are your specific goals, what projects do you have laid out for yourself? What do you need to enable you to do your best this year? Do you need equipment, do you need volunteers, do you need assistance, do you need finances, do you need time and discipline, or is there something else?

As you can see, part of the constructive approach of these pastors involves asking questions designed to lean forward, while still providing opportunity to discuss past performance.

Must Be Culturally Informed—While there are multiple approaches for facilitating staff reviews (see appendix A), it is unwise to think that "one size fits all" when it comes to your own process. Every ministry organization has its own history, values, and surrounding community culture. Such particularities have a big effect on how working relationships and assessments are handled.

A recent article highlighted how in one Asian country, there isn't even a word in their language for "feedback" because it isn't something anyone does. The notion is this: "If you don't hear from your manager, you're doing well. If your manager asks for an update on your project, that means you're not doing well" (see appendix A, BBC News).

Wherever you serve, it is important to let the cultural nuances inform your method of staff review. This pastor reports the relationship between their church culture and performance assessment:

> We have this value, this bias I guess, that plays into the staff values. It's an issue of culture and strategy. We have this belief that culture eats strategy for breakfast. What I mean by that is you can have all the right strategy, all the right business stuff, but to us actually culture is important. Culture basically deals with the way we do things. Strategy might actually be the things you do. We just think that creating culture is the thing that comes first, and it's the more important thing.

Generational differences are a part of this cultural awareness and can pose a challenge as supervisors try to adjust to the unique working styles of their often younger staff members. This adjustment goes both ways, of course, and should be factored into expectations and job descriptions, as necessary. One senior pastor shares this experience:

> These days we are dealing with millennial staffers whose way of doing things are so different than us baby boomer pastors. For example, a wonderful youth pastor, only 26 years old with so much upside to his ministry left our church less than a year after hiring because he thought my approach to the staff was too rigid for him to function. As a half-timer, I demanded certain office hours but he felt trapped working in the church office. He wanted more freedom of time in his ministry.

Must Be Personalized—Culture is, indeed, a significant factor in implementing effective staff reviews, but alongside that comes the impact of making sure you take into consideration the personality, strengths, gifts, areas of weakness, and other tendencies of your ministry colleagues. In the preceding chapters, we have emphasized the importance of knowing your team, of establishing a growing knowledge of them as individuals. The depth of your relationship with your direct reports relates significantly to the helpfulness of their review. One pastor shares openly how keeping the process personal allows room for imperfection, while giving others on the team opportunity to complement his ministry through their strengths:

> *We do annual staff reviews that reflect back our ministry values. We allow the staff to articulate which were the values they really strongly lock into, and which are the ones that are more difficult for them to manage. So for me, one of my least would be excellence . . . and my staff knows that. They know that I need help slowing down and allowing someone to proofread my stuff before it goes out. I'm not particularly good at that. As a staff we have the freedom to admit, "these are the things I feel like I'm firing on all cylinders on, that I'm doing really well, and these are some of my least-best growth area kinds of things." Because nobody's going to be a 10 on all of these, right?*

Must Be Safe—When the staff review process is free of unfair comparisons, a sense of safety emerges. People can fail without fear of losing their positions, as this pastor recalls from his staff experience:

> *God provided a wonderful situation for my wife and I and our young family to grow up in ministry. I learned by doing and I had plenty of opportunity to do and fail. He didn't get in the way of that. . . . I never felt like my head was on the chopping block in terms of performance. That if I didn't perform or get the right results in a ministry that I was done or under evaluation.*

Aside from the freedom to fail, keeping salaries separate from staff reviews is highly recommended by many experts. While tying pay to performance is certainly a big part of some professions (e.g., car sales), pastoral ministry is about goals more difficult to measure (spiritual maturity in its various manifestations). One supervisor reports his efforts to keep salary and performance apart:

> *The budget committee wanted to give my staff person a raise of 20%. But it was because he was poorly paid. Some people kind of reacted to it and turned it into a performance question. There wasn't a performance issue, and there hadn't been one at all until the money was on the table, and so that was where it was like "well you just can't do that folks, those are two different things. And the one seems to be substituting for the other, you just don't like it." So I try to advocate for them in those things.*

Maintaining confidentiality is another way to keep the review process safe. What happens during the review must stay in the room—between the supervisor and the staff person. One of our respondents shares a situation where such is not the case:

> *One thing that has lessened my feeling supported is hearing the supervising pastor critique the work of other employees. Of course the pastor is sweet*

normally to those employees, so to hear criticism behind closed doors makes me suspicious.

Must Be Honest—When safety is present, honesty can enter in. Often, in pastoral settings, supervisors and the staff they lead can be too polite, sugar-coating the truth for fear of offending or seeming "unchristian." Being gracious toward one another is virtuous, but it must be in the vein of what the apostle Paul calls "speaking the truth in love" (Ephesians 4:15), as he demonstrates when challenging believers to remain strong in their faith. This staff person comments on a trait he does *not* appreciate in how his immediate supervisor handles staff reviews:

> *Not providing concrete suggestions and feedback with my challenges. Every-thing seems to be "good." I can use more honest feedback and some sugges-tions from his experiences.*

During staff reviews, supervisors should welcome feedback from their staff concerning their own effectiveness as a team leader. Being able to receive input from our staff requires that we are willing to receive it. One pastor shares why supervisors sometimes struggle with this:

> *Often I find supervisors who are either lacking self-awareness, or they're insecure, and they really aren't open to honest feedback. I think we say that a lot, but I've seen so many supervisors who shut people down, make it really obvious that their feedback isn't welcome. And I think that is a tremendous miss for us as supervisors when we can't hear the honest evaluation or hear the hard thing from the people who work for us. Whenever that begins to happen, our response in the first thirty seconds is going to set the tone, for how much we're really going to be open to that.*

Must Be Liberating—It is typical for us to associate the review process with control. We are responsible for performing our jobs, and our supervisors decide if we've fulfilled our obligations at the annual review. One pastor reflects:

> *I think the challenge overseeing pastors have is balancing intervention with freedom. I've had both negligence and micromanaging. Neither allowed me to grow. In those seasons in which I'm given freedom to chart a course and also accountability to someone more experienced than myself, I feel supported.*

The review process is one of the best times to be encouraged to dream and cast vision. Our university review protocol includes an entire section in which we share our aspirations. Another pastor remarks how this is incorpo-rated into their staff reviews:

We do this annual plan now, where staff come up with what their vision is for next year, what some monthly goals are, and then we just stick with those measurable goals throughout the year. That has helped a lot with keeping me on track, and keeping them accountable.

Must Be Developmental—Approaching staff reviews as an opportunity to look forward cultivates an environment where personal development and growth is encouraged. This certainly characterizes one pastor's situation:

We really try to have this culture where we don't just see you as a person who's here to help us accomplish the vision of the church, we care about you and want you to grow.

In chapter 6, we looked at staff development in terms of helping our colleagues explore and prepare for their life calling—the long view. Here we will listen to the wisdom effective supervising pastors share concerning how their staff can be better trained and developed to thrive in their current ministry positions.

STAFF DEVELOPMENT

It is a common mistake. Ministries hire people to do a job, thinking they have all the training and abilities necessary to excel. While expecting competence in our staff team is fair, it is important to cultivate an environment of ongoing ministry skill development and perspective. This pastor's staff team reflects this notion:

We had all our leaders read The Twenty-one Irrefutable Laws of Leadership [1] *together. Then we got the DVD teaching set and offered that during the summer. We selected a few of the laws and watched together with people who signed up . . . and discussed it around tables. We've had this culture of trying to develop ourselves, our abilities. Our children's ministry leader goes to a children's pastors conference . . . we don't go to that one with her, but we ask her when she comes back to share some of the things that she got out of it and that maybe the church needs to be aware of.*

The supervising pastors in our research group highlight several strategies that encourage staff in developing their competence and fulfillment in their areas of service (table 7.2):

Know Your People—In chapter 6, we highlight the importance of establishing solid relationships with members of your staff team. Getting to know your colleagues starts when they're hired, but ought to continue throughout their tenure. Accept them for who they are, for how God has crafted them, and provide appropriate opportunities for personal growth. One lead pastor

Table 7.2.   Strategies for Staff Development

Know your people

Encourage risk

Invest time and money

Celebrate growth

Maximize staff meetings

Be a model and mentor

Be a coach

remembers how a former supervisor's lack of such understanding hindered his ministerial growth and zeal:

> *My head pastor forced me to go to certain prayer locations and/or training seminars that I was not comfortable with (I am a conservative Presbyterian and he is Pentecostal). He should have let me be when I constantly declined, but he wouldn't have any of it. He hired me whilst knowing I was so conservative. If he was okay with that, then why was he constantly trying to force me to change? This hindered me from growth and made me dislike my ministry more.*

Another shares how knowing your colleagues engenders a very positive working relationship:

> *My supervisor appreciated the complement that we were to one another in our gifting and abilities. That also helped me in taking responsibility in that I saw how God had put us together to help the church be effective in our mission.*

We show our care for our staff people when the growth opportunities we provide are in keeping with their unique qualities and needs. A deepening relationship leads the way in this regard.

Encourage Risk—This advice will threaten you if control is the driving force in your relationship with staff. If you can keep that in balance, however, and give your colleagues room to try new things, solid growth often ensues:

> *My supervising pastor had the where-with-all to train me and then give me the space and freedom to run with any responsibility given to me. He allowed me opportunity to be creative, risk doing something new, work things out in my own mind and to even fail at specific tasks.*

A former staff member at a very large church benefited from this approach:

A big thing I learned there was that the senior pastor was always willing to take a risk and do on-the-job training, as opposed to forcing people to jump through a lot of hoops or get a lot of certification before they do anything. He was much more willing to push people into the deep end than try to come alongside them and help them learn how to swim. It shaped my approach to supervision a little bit in terms of believing in people but also being willing to take risks and hire people who maybe don't have all the boxes checked [and give them] a chance to take on something and be empowered to try something new.

Several of our respondents shared how they advanced in their ministries while staying in their present church or other ministry context. The effect of being allowed to venture out into new territory, where they could fail and still be supported, was to see their careers blossom in ways never imagined.

Personally, the most growth-inducing time in my years here at the seminary was when I was tapped to lead a large grant-funded program. During the five years this program was running, my wife, who served as associate director, and I learned all kinds of new skills, and were exposed to a new world of ideas and relationships that still benefit us today, over thirteen years later. We would not have sought this challenge, but our dean, who knew us well, saw this as a beneficial step for us in our ministry together.

Invest Time and Money—Great supervisors are known for being generous investors in their colleagues' ministry lives. Perhaps the most precious resource we can give is time. Maybe you have been blessed like this pastor:

My lead pastor wasn't big on the yearly reviews and things like that. But what he was good at was maximizing time. If he was going to a meeting across town, he would grab myself, one of the other pastors, and make the most of the ride over. His style was much more caught than taught. Spending quality time with him was great . . . he seized the moment.

Often money must be spent to secure helpful resources for staff growth. Several ideas are mentioned through our interviews and survey:

If a staff person comes in and says, "I'd like to go to this conference," we'll find the money for it because it's a value.

When we've done developmental things for just the staff; had in speakers, even videos from conferences, team times . . . when the church has done that, it's been very effective. Because it breaks you out of your individual focus in ministry, and takes you to that more visionary, personal growth that you really need to thrive in ministry.

We want to home-grow our staff. We want to be a place that grows future pastors, missionaries, and Christian leaders. So we established a line of support between seventy and a hundred thousand dollars in scholarship money *for people who are in school. So if you're from our church and you're going off to school, and you apply, we'll give you a $1,000 scholarship.*

In addition, it's helpful to provide funds so your staff can join guilds related to their field, or subscribe to publications that will enhance their professional effectiveness. And don't forget time off and funds to help them attend related gatherings.

Celebrate Growth—This pastor's reflection says it all:

In my previous church, I served as a stand-in Worship Director. I was not paid, but was serving as a pastoral intern and fulfilling the role. Because I was in seminary at the time, and felt overwhelmed and burdened often, my Senior Pastor did a great job of encouraging me where he saw areas of growth, and what I was doing well, especially when I was discouraged. He affirmed me where he liked the decisions I made (such as song selections, worship flow, team member selection, etc.). He would even make it a point to honor and encourage me from the pulpit when it proved a point of illustration or application for his sermons. My supervising pastor has encouraged me specifically where he has seen growth and what I have done well. He has also allowed me freedom to think through how to make decisions, or even change things when necessary.

This supervisor certainly encourages risk (see above), but he goes beyond that to celebrating and honoring his staff as it is occurring. Supportive lead pastors can also arrange parties for staff who graduate from learning programs, or who have demonstrated a new level of expertise in any particular area of their responsibilities. It takes little energy but demonstrates the value you put on personal professional growth.

Maximize Staff Meetings—Kevin has addressed staff meetings in chapters 3 and 4, and here we simply present the notion that development of staff members can have a place in what is usually a full agenda. These regular get-togethers can foster growth in many ways. Here are a couple of ideas from our respondents:

Then there's a section of the staff meeting that's designated to promote growth or development. Sometimes we will read a book together, and we'll talk about the book that we're all reading as a staff, in order to keep us growing and being sharpened. We have this mantra where we say, "Growing people grow people."

Some of these conversations we have in staff meetings are like "why am I talking about how we're doing baptism since I'm not going to be doing the baptism," or "why are we talking about this budget thing?" So we remind them that this is part of your training, this is part of church work, this is part of understanding what the church is about. Figuring out how people perceive

*things differently, and what we need to be concerned about and what we don't
need to be concerned about . . . this helps us all grow.*

Be a Model and Mentor—Whether we accept it or not, we are models
and mentors to our staff. It's not a question of "if" but one of whether we are
willing to assume the role and allow it to encourage our staff. Staff families
are developed through the example of our families, as one pastor appreciates
about a former supervisor:

> *Being able to observe their family, marriage and ministry life modeled for us
> significant ways to take responsibility for ministry, family responsibilities and
> growth. They modeled good boundaries and just being real people in ministry.
> They also modeled hearts for the Lord and living lives of mission . . . how to
> parent, be in ministry, deal with hard things in ministry . . . practical stuff.*

Another highlights these benefits:

> *My supervising pastor modeled for me what it looks like to work hard, love
> others, and think through administrative/organizational issues. Sometimes he
> would share with me insight into what he was doing and this helped me see
> how I might do things better or differently.*

In terms of mentoring, which informally goes on within modeling, this pastor
makes an insightful point regarding what has been most helpful in developing his role:

> *I really think mentorship is the main thing. Because they walk with you in life,
> they walk through situations with you, being able to phone them, meet in
> person, text message, even e-mail . . . here's the situation—what do you think?*

Be a Coach—An approach for developing staff that some effective
supervisors prefer is that of coaching. This highlights the progression in
which the supervisor may play along with the team in order to train and
illustrate good technique, but ultimately desires them to stand on their own
by game day. Such is the experience of this fortunate player:

> *Early on when I was a youth pastor my pastor would take me on hospital
> visits, or where we were in Virginia we'd do a little more home visits too. And
> he would take me and just kind of coach me before we went in, and give me
> feedback after we had a visit to the hospital. Just got comfortable making
> hospital visits and people who were obviously in crisis, or people who wanted
> to sit down and discuss spiritual questions or issues, chances to share your
> faith. So I learned a lot from just shadowing him and him giving me opportu-
> nities to join in the conversation too, because I was pretty green.*

The benefits of good coaching can also include more than the personal growth of the staff, as suggested by this minister:

> *I'd say learn to think like a coach, not a player. I think that's a huge mindset shift you have to have when you supervise people. Because players make plays, but coaches make players, and what you're trying to do is make a great player . . . and to realize that the success of that staff member actually multiplies their ministry, sometimes tenfold.*

SOME FINAL CONSIDERATIONS

Well-administered staff reviews facilitate staff effectiveness and development. A few key decisions must be made in this process:

Frequency/Timing of Reviews—Most of our respondents report annual reviews for staff. New staff members often receive more frequent reviews (six months) as they acclimate to their new ministry contexts and responsibilities.

Participants in Reviews—While many supervisors indicated that their reviews included only them and their staff person, it is also suggested by some that a senior pastor may be included, as well as an elder. It is important to note, however, that if other individuals are included, it may be perceived as some sort of inquisition. So it is always important to clearly explain why particular people are included in any review.

The so-called 360-degree review is sometimes used to assess staff members. In this approach, eight to ten colleagues (paid and volunteer) rate the staff person anonymously on any number of traits. While this can perhaps give a more objective picture of how a staff person is functioning, it should be used with great care as it can instill a lack of trust among the team members. We don't recommend it for most situations.

Questions for Reviews—Staff reviews require asking the right questions. The Baptist General Conference of Texas provides the following sample list (which is usually given to the staff before the face-to-face interview) on its website (see appendix A):

1. List your primary accomplishments this evaluation period.
2. Explain any challenges you encountered that affected your work or performance in this evaluation period.
3. What critical skills/strengths/relationships have you built (or improved) and applied?
4. What critical skills/strengths/relationships would you like to develop for the next evaluation period?
5. Is your current workload reasonable? What adjustments in workload would you suggest?

6. What changes, if any, are needed to make your job description accurately reflect your current responsibilities?
7. How can the other staff persons better help you to accomplish your goals/tasks in the future?
8. Explain any processes/procedures/tasks that you would like to discuss with your supervisor that would enhance the success of your work. Address other comments you have.

Additional resources are available in appendix A, including helpful Internet sites and articles that will give you excellent ideas as you develop or enhance your approach to reviewing your staff and encouraging growth in their areas of service.

TAKING INVENTORY

Staff reviews and staff development can be a challenge both for supervisors and those they supervise. We've unpacked some important principles and practices above and discussed ways to help staff members grow and develop in their ministries. The following questions can be a helpful chance for you to assess your review procedures and get the perspectives of your associate staff on what would make the procedures more beneficial for them as well. Take time to identify the issues that may be most helpful to focus on, and then work through the relevant questions and identify what is going well in your setting, and what needs attention to make reviews a more positive and beneficial experience.

Staff Reviews

Leader: Are staff reviews part of my approach to supervision? If not, what might be some key reasons they are not being done?

With Your Associates: In your opinion, why are staff reviews not a part of our team experience here? If we developed reviews, what ideas would you like to share in shaping them?

Leader: What resources are available to begin the process of developing staff reviews?

With Your Associates: In previous staff settings, have you found a certain approach to staff reviews effective and encouraging? Could you secure information from your previous supervisor regarding his or her approach?

Leader: How often should reviews be conducted within our ministry context and with these particular staff members? Is annually often enough, or should we plan them for every six months? More often still?

With Your Associates: Ideally, how often would you like to engage in staff reviews? Are there times of the ministry year when they would be most helpful? How many times a year is ideal, in your opinion?

Leader: Am I keeping good records of my interactions with staff? Are all important meetings documented and kept in a secured location?

With Your Associates: Are you comfortable with me keeping written records of staff reviews? Are you aware of why it is important we do so? What are your concerns regarding this practice? Can you think of helpful safeguards that will ensure that this information is kept confidential?

Leader: Are there ways we can incorporate staff review within the working culture we already have established (i.e., regular staff meetings, debriefing sessions held after major events or milestones)?

With Your Associates: Do you think it is possible to include staff reviews within the context of our regular staff meetings? What are your concerns about such an idea? Would brief one-on-one interactions after regular meetings be helpful or not? Would you feel free to ask for an impromptu personal review, should you feel it beneficial? What would prevent you from asking for this?

Leader: Do we have clear and realistic job descriptions? Are staff members fully aware of the expectations I have of them?

With Your Associates: Tell me how you feel about your job description. What aspects of it are unclear and most often cause misunderstanding? How is it unfair or unrealistic, in your opinion? What would your ideal job description look like? Am I clear in what I expect from you, and are you comfortable with that? Tell me more.

Leader: Have we done well in establishing goals and timelines for our projects? Can staff members clearly state our mission and vision?

With Your Associates: As your supervisor, am I helpful and effective in assisting you in setting goals and timelines for your programs? How could I be a better provider in this area?

Do we all have a clear understanding of our mission and vision? Is our published version of these items well worded or vague? What would you suggest to make them more powerful?

Leader: Are our staff reviews characterized by robust discussion, open exchange of ideas and assessments? During these reviews, do I ask good questions and listen carefully to those whom I supervise?

With Your Associates: Do you feel free to discuss everything about your ministry during our staff reviews? What areas of discussion are difficult to bring up, and why do you think this is so? What question(s) would you wish I asked during your staff review? How could I make our reviews more conducive to openness and freedom of expression?

Leader: Is there anything about the local community or church culture that can inform me as to how staff review should be administered? How do people communicate here, what is the acceptable mode of confronting subordinates when things aren't going as well as hoped?

With Your Associates: Can you share with me any particular aspects of staff reviews that are affected by the cultural characteristics of this church . . . this community . . . this general region? How can I be more culturally sensitive as your supervisor? How can I change my approach to staff reviews that will enhance their effectiveness in light of our present cultural context?

Leader: Am I personalizing my staff reviews? What is unique about my colleagues, their abilities, perspectives, history, spiritual gifts, work styles, and weaknesses that can inform the process of evaluating their performance? Do I subconsciously compare my staff to one another unfairly?

With Your Associates: Do you feel that I understand your unique gifts, abilities, personality, and personal history well enough to provide fair and informed reviews of your work? What am I missing, and can you lead me to a better understanding of you as a person and coworker? Have I made you feel as though I'm comparing you to others on staff? How do I do this, and what can I do to alleviate that impression?

Leader: Is there any way in which I may not be keeping our staff reviews confidential? How can I protect the interactions I have with my colleagues during and after performance reviews? How is documentation of these reviews securely stored? Who has access to them?

With Your Associates: Do you ever feel that our discussions make it outside this room? What leads you to this conclusion when you sense this is the case? What can I do to assure you of the privacy of your staff reviews?

Leader: Are our staff reviews characterized by honesty? Can we share openly and without fear of recrimination on this team? What might be hindering us in knowing a deeper sense of trust within our team?

With Your Associates: Are there areas where you struggle with being honest during our staff review process? Can you identify and share with me the reason(s) for this? What kinds of settings would encourage you (us) to engage in an open exchange of hearts and minds? (e.g., extended retreats . . . half days on campus prayer and share mini-retreats?)

Leader: Do I tend to be too easy on the staff? Do I avoid saying the hard things when they are necessary? If so, why?

With Your Associates: Do you feel I'm too easy or casual with you during your staff reviews? Are there areas of accountability I should pay more attention to that would help you be more productive and fulfilled in your ministry area? What one question would you bring up if you were administering your own staff review?

Leader: Do I struggle with having to control everything that goes on in the team? Do my staff reviews feel like inquisitions instead of opportunities to give and take and explore new ways of realizing our shared goals and vision?

With Your Associates: Am I a micromanager? If so, what leads you to that opinion? How could I change my approach to these reviews that would help you relax and enjoy and benefit from the process more?

Leader: Do I ask my staff to share their hopes and dreams about their area of ministry? When they do, is it received respectfully and taken seriously by me and other leaders?

With Your Associates: What are your dreams and aspirations for your ministry? Paint me a picture of what you envision for the next year. How can I be a cheerleader for you and resource you in pursuit of your dreams?

Staff Development

Leader: As I get to know my staff, am I looking for suitable avenues through which they can grow in their professional abilities and enlarge their perspective on ministry? Do I consult with them in determining the best options?

With Your Associates: What kinds of growth opportunities would be encouraging to you right now? Could you determine the time and money it would cost to pursue these avenues? Are there details and rationale you could provide that would help me in securing these resources for you?

Leader: Is risk a part of the DNA of how our team operates? Do I encourage it? If not, why not?

With Your Associates: What wild and crazy ideas do you have concerning your ministry area? What has kept you and us from trying out one or more of these ideas? Is there history in this ministry that prevents us from taking some risks? What can we learn from our past in trying new ideas going forward?

Leader: How can I make risk taking a part of my staff review process? What must I do to create an environment where colleagues feel safe to try new things, even if they fail?

With Your Associates: As you look ahead to a new year, what would you like to try that is new and perhaps even revolutionary? What would you need from me in order to engage in this attempt at something new? What obstacles can we anticipate, and how might we together address these in order to make progress while still showing sensitivity to our entire congregation? Are you willing to accept some push-back and misunderstanding?

Leader: Am I looking out for ways my staff can stretch their personal horizons while enhancing their particular area of service on the team?

With Your Associates: Share with me something you've often thought would be a great step forward in your ministry career development. If it's education, what sort of program would motivate you? What kinds of resources would you need to realize any such step forward?

Leader: Is there money available to purchase resources for our staff? If not now, what can we do to make that happen?

With Your Associates: Could you give me a prioritized wish list of resources that would enhance your ministry area? Are there ways in which your area budget could be reallocated to provide for some of these items?

Leader: Have I asked my staff members what they would appreciate in terms of resources for their growth in ministry effectiveness (conferences, guild memberships, books, seminars)?

With Your Associates: Do you know of particular conferences, guilds, printed resources, and seminars that are focused on your area of ministry responsibility? If we were able to provide some funding for these resources, which of them would be a priority to you at this time? Would you do some research and come back with a few possibilities that would excite you?

Leader: What are we doing to encourage further education within our staff? Is tuition assistance possible, and if not, how can we begin to secure funding?

With Your Associates: Have you ever thought of obtaining additional education? In which area of study are you most interested? What, if anything, has kept you from pursuing this goal until now? Would you be willing to articulate a case for the pursuit of your dreams and aspirations in this regard in writing—for the record and for purposes of promotion among board members, with your permission?

Leader: Do I keep track of the "wins" my staff experience, and make those part of the review process?

With Your Associates: How could we best celebrate the victories within our various areas of ministry? What could I do to promote your work without embarrassing you? Have I missed something in the past that made you feel unappreciated? Will you agree to make sure I know about your wins as they are savored?

Leader: How can we utilize our staff meetings for growth and development? Should this be a regular feature, or something we focus on once every quarter?

With Your Associates: In your memory, what aspect(s) of our regular staff meetings have been most beneficial and encouraging to you? Are there features of our staff meetings that could better be handled one-on-one, saving time for other items? What would those items be? What area(s) of your personal and professional development are most desired right now, and how could we provide some of that during our staff meetings? Should we focus on staff development monthly, quarterly, semiannually?

Leader: Have I been aware of the influence I have with staff as a mentor and model to them? Am I missing any opportunities to share my life and ministry?

With Your Associates: Does my leadership and life example provide a positive influence upon you and those you serve? Where can I do a better job as a mentor and model? Are there times and places where you wished I was there to share more of my life and ministry with you?

Leader: In what activities could I bring staff along and use the opportunity to demonstrate ministry skills and share wisdom with them (and them with me)?

With Your Associates: What kind of pastoral activities in my job description would be interesting for you to observe and even participate in with me? Could you identify a few opportunities where I could shadow you and learn more of your ministry and the people you serve?

Leader: Can I see myself as a coach, someone who makes players, not just my own plays? Am I interested in developing the staff personally and professionally, or only concerned about their performance in their particular staff position?

With Your Associates: Have you sensed in me a sincere desire to see you succeed in your life and ministry? In what ways could I be better at communicating that desire to you? Are there areas of your ministry where I have not been the best coach for you? When do I run on the field and try to make the play for you? Do you feel treasured as a gifted colleague? If not, how can I better communicate that to you?

Chapter Eight

Letting Go—Staff Transitions

Mick Boersma

Part of my faculty responsibility includes directing our seminary placement office. In the last thirty years, I've seen a lot of the good, bad, and ugly of pastoral transition. I help graduates find their first assignment, but spend most of my time assisting veterans find their way through the labyrinth of ministry searches and candidacy. Transition is a big factor in pastoral careers, due to the frequency with which ministerial staff change positions.

You've most likely seen the so-called statistics—that huge numbers of ministers are calling it quits and leaving ministry altogether. More reliable researchers are questioning this perception. Lifeway Christian Resources, one of the world's largest providers of ministry support, and well-known for its accurate research, reports these five top reasons pastors are abandoning the pastorate:

1. Change of calling (37 percent)
2. Conflict in a church (26 percent)
3. Family issues (17 percent)
4. Burnout (10 percent)
5. Personal finances (8 percent)[1]

On the brighter side, however, they also report that many ministers, while being challenged in their callings, are not quitting, but pursuing their ministries with purpose and fulfillment. They are moving around, finding new venues and expressions of ministry service. And some research indicates these moves are being made on average every three to five years. Reasons for changing ministry settings are varied, with the most prevalent being:

1. I took the church as far as I could (54 percent);

2. my family needed a change (34 percent);
3. there was conflict in the ministry (23 percent);
4. the church did not embrace my approach to ministry (19 percent);
5. the church had unrealistic expectations (18 percent);
6. it was not a good fit (18 percent);
7. I was reassigned (18 percent);
8. I was asked to leave (8 percent). [2]

Our research affirms these and includes a few more:

> *We have two other guys who are relatively new . . . and both of them just* **began doing illegal things**. *As we understand the qualifications for elders and pastors, that's disqualifying.*

> *Well, in one church we served,* **with the guy who was dishonest**, *after one of those, my wife said "we're done here . . . we're transitioning."*

> *Our music guy ended up going down a direction where he was* **getting lazy**, *and was very much concerned about a performance on Sunday morning rather than leading the congregation.*

Ministry supervision can sometimes mean helping your staff move on. This can mean shifting positions within their present ministry, helping them move along to a new opportunity, or even letting them go due to various circumstances. Regardless of the rationale, our surveys and interviews have highlighted the importance of navigating this aspect of supervision thoughtfully and carefully.

THE GOLDEN RULE OF STAFF TRANSITIONS

Most supervising pastors we talked to had personal experience transitioning between ministries. In some cases, that move was painful. In reflecting on their comments, these words from Jesus aptly convey their sentiments.

> So whatever you wish that others would do to you, do also to them, for this is the Law and the Prophets. (Matthew 7:12)

In dealing with staff transitions, Jesus's command serves as a powerful rule of thumb in navigating this aspect of leadership. And like personally supporting staff (chapter 6), effective leadership in this endeavor is well within reach. However, we would submit that in order to reflect the heart of Christ, any approach taken should embrace the following eight basic commitments (table 8.1):

Table 8.1. The Golden Rule of Staff Transitions: Eight Basic Commitments

Be patient

Be communicative

Be honest

Be well-intentioned

Be consistent

Be generous

Be kind

Be reflective

Be Patient—My dad was a farmer in the great state of Iowa. He was a wise and caring father and husband, faithful church elder, and successful agriculturalist. He taught me a lot of great life principles, including "make haste, make waste," and "do it right the first time." While he struggled at times being patient, he knew its value in the affairs of life. Patience saved us a lot of work, expense, and regret on our family farm. You'll want to approach this whole business of terminations the same way. So here's a life lesson I'll pass along to you: "Go slow in letting people go."

People's lives are at stake. And there is a high cost to be paid for acting hastily. One ministry coach reviewed several studies regarding employee turnover and found the financial cost to congregations at 20–22 percent of the salary of the person being replaced. This included severance pay, lost membership, lost contributions, the cost of an interim, lost productivity, and the drain on remaining staff (Cal Habig, valuedrivenleaders.org, see appendix A).

Additionally, I would mention the effect on the one leaving and on staff morale and the potential loss of trust in the ministry leadership, including the senior staff and elder board. Granted, many transitions are healthy for both the staff person and the ministry they leave behind. But even then, transitions are unsettling and should be approached with great care and patience. One pastor reflects this concern:

> *I think one of the big things for me is helping elder boards understand the real price of turnover . . . what it means in terms of lost institutional knowledge . . . the actual transition of someone out and the interim time when you're trying to find the right person . . . and you're taking a risk in "are you actually going to get the right person?"*

Be Communicative—Assuming you have engaged meaningfully with your staff from the start by clearly defining job expectations (see chapter 2), supervisors must cultivate a working environment in which open and honest feedback is the norm. One oft-heard complaint by staff members who have been let go is reflected by this former associate:

> It was only when I was informed that I would not be renewed did my supervising pastor share with me his thoughts about my job performance; and most of his information came from biased sources. I had never felt so unfairly treated by the church leadership in my life, and for a while caused me to struggle with bitterness against certain individuals.

The supervisor-staff relationship should be one of regular conversation concerning ministry expectations, goals, and performance. It should never come as a shock when someone is informed they will be let go. An atmosphere of transparency prevents such trauma, even though pain is often still present. Effective communication is something all ministry staff should work on together all the time.

A critical part of this communication involves keeping accurate records. Staff meetings should be chronicled for later reference. Agreements, commitments, and job performance reviews must be documented. In the future, these records will be helpful in mapping your course of understanding and action with your colleagues. They also will serve as a guide to note progress, or the lack thereof, in any difficult discussions that might lead to a termination.

If a staff member is let go, communicating this decision starts with that staff person. The staff member's colleagues (paid and volunteer staff) should be informed soon after, and if necessary, the entire congregation. Enough information should be provided so as to minimize speculation, yet protect confidentiality.

Last, be sure to plan an exit interview. Once a decision has been made to transition one of the staff, it is helpful to converse about the experience they have had, hear of the blessings and difficulties they experienced during their tenure, and note ideas they would suggest to make improvements. While some of this may be hard to hear, it honors your staff person to listen and speaks to your wisdom and grace in receiving their input. Realize, however, that it is possible the staff member will not be able or willing to be interviewed, especially when the termination is forced. In addition to you and the staff member, it might be appropriate and helpful for the senior pastor and a member of the elder board to participate in this interview.

Considerations and examples of the types of questions to ask are well presented in an article by Warren Lynn, Executive Minister for Christian Vocations, Disciples Home Missions (a ministry of the Disciples of Christ) (see appendix A).

Be Honest—We've considered what makes for healthy staff reviews in chapter 7. Among other points, they should be fair, open, free of hidden agendas, and part of the regular office calendar. And if along the way things aren't working out, good supervisors assist staff in determining if another path would be more fruitful. One pastor reflects:

> *My experience is that the staff person . . . if there's something that they're not very good at or they resist doing . . . you're just not going to be able to change them.*

In his case, the "letting go" was mostly the result of making a bad hire in the first place (see chapter 2). Sometimes it is quite difficult to know the long-term compatibility of a minister with his or her area of responsibility. Once that becomes apparent, either the staff member should be encouraged and equipped to adjust or be assisted in the search for a more appropriate service setting.

A part of being honest is making the hard decision to terminate someone. Pretending a situation is okay when it is not does justice to no one. Leaders who confidently, yet thoughtfully, handle such a challenge are appreciated most of the time, even by the individual released from a job. One pastor recalls his experience:

> *I'm not quick to conclude there's no hope in a situation . . . by the time I've concluded it other people are sure. So I have found that in each case where I've needed to act and say it's time to let this one go, I think I've ended up with greater respect. I've had more status by the time the thing was over, because people respected the fact that I would face it and would do it.*

In this process, helping your associates ask themselves the right questions is critical. Relational, organizational, familial, congregational, emotional, and professional areas of inquiry must be frankly addressed. Each of these categories includes a number of important questions. A thorough list can be found in *Moving On Moving Forward; A Guide for Pastors in Transition.*[3] The result of such honest discussion may well lead to a fresh chapter of service in their current ministry. But it could also provide helpful perspective for a staff member who needs to move on.

Be Well-Intentioned—Fear of job loss is often acute in ministry contexts. Few staff members have financial reserves to see them through a transition, unless a new position awaits them. As well, there is the grief of losing friends, since ministers leave a community, not just a job. Staff who are in the midst of transition need to believe their supervisor is leading with a heart of compassion and understanding—and is not someone who will cut them off at the knees. As one senior pastor notes:

> *I find it fascinating, especially with associate staff, and I haven't been able to solve it, it's still a head-scratcher for me, but the fear of being fired is very real . . . in my experience the associate staff really need to know that they are*

secure in their position, aside from a moral or a legal failure . . . that I the senior pastor really do have their back.

When a staff member is convinced his or her supervisor wants the best for them, that their intentions are only for their good, transitions can foster growth and hope, even in the midst of loss. One university human resources director sums up his many years of staff management:

If you tell staff the full story, do your best for them, they can handle being laid off.

My mentor, Wally, is well known for what many of his protégés call his "Wallyisms." One such slice of wisdom goes like this:

If people get the idea you are just using them for your own personal aspirations, you will lose them and never get them back.

In the pressure of supervising others toward vision and goals, this attitude can easily develop. The person becomes less important than the task, and colleagues become convinced they are just a means to an end. Our good intentions toward co-laborers will be conveyed in the way we work with them through times of transition.

Be Consistent—Few things dishearten a staff more than inequity. Treating people differently with regard to performance standards, compensation, or termination procedures is a recipe for disaster. To help prevent such chaos, ministries are well advised to develop policy manuals. While they may limit some flexibility in handling unique situations, a clear and consistent set of guidelines can only help foster a healthy environment within a staff.

Of course, if you have a policy manual, it is important to follow it. More than a few ministries have spent time and effort constructing an effective procedural document, only to keep it in a file drawer and forget to use it. Policies should be made available to all staff members, and updated as necessary. Many examples are available on the Internet simply by entering "church employee manual" or some such descriptor. Denominational resources may be available, as well.

While less frequent than some public perception might imply, there are occasions when character failure is at the heart of a pastoral termination. In such instances, congregations with a clear policy concerning church discipline should follow that course with a staff person, as they would with any church member. Best practices in setting up effective, fair, and consistent disciplinary procedures for staff (and all congregation members) include:

• teaching regularly about the disciplinary role of the church;

- explaining to new staff the requirements of their commitment and the potential for discipline if they breach them;
- asking new associates to sign an agreement and including references to the right of the church to discipline;
- being consistent in the enforcement of church law;
- carefully following church disciplinary procedures;
- carefully protecting the privacy of the individuals involved in the process;
- not allowing unsubstantiated charges to be made public;
- basing disciplinary decisions on biblical grounds and framing them that way;
- if appropriate, publicly conveying a disciplinary decision, being certain it can be fully substantiated and basing the publication on biblical grounds.

Consistency is also important in dealing with cases of poor staff performance. A helpful procedure and related considerations are expertly conveyed in another Alban book, *When Moses Meets Aaron* (Rendle and Beaumont, 2007; see appendix A). Clear and uniform procedures not only provide a plan for action when things go wrong, more importantly they can prevent unfortunate situations from developing in the first place.

Be Generous—In my position as a placement director, I am often saddened by the attitude of certain ministries in search of new leadership. Often they ask a question like this: "How much do youth pastors (add any ministry position) make these days?" Not giving them a figure, I'll ask them where the church is, whether they want the pastor's spouse to have to work, what decent housing costs, what kind of health insurance will be provided, what sort of expense account will be available, and the manner of retirement savings they may contribute to their next leader.

Not surprisingly, there is usually silence on the other end of the line. That's because many ministries are not focused on fully supporting their new pastor, but only want to know the least amount they can offer and still get some response from potential candidates. This may sound cynical, but it is too often the case. As we interact with lead pastors, the notion of generosity is often mentioned, which makes their context of pastoral ministry one of greater joy and contentment. As one senior pastor says:

> . . . *with the whole staff in the financial area, I think we do as well as any church supporting them at the level that might make it hard for them to leave.*

A ministry that diligently works at being generous in salary, benefits, and working conditions will continue that spirit when helping a staff member as they move along. While some terminations are more difficult than others, love and care should be conveyed to all God's servants as they leave.

In terms of providing financial support, severance should be considered. While not legally required, it is appropriate in cases where staff is asked to leave due to changes beyond their control, or when they have no position waiting for them. A generous policy would stipulate two weeks' salary for each year of service.

Unless the staff person is moving to another job with sufficient benefits, the consideration of helping them pay for health care costs is also appropriate, whether through a program like COBRA or with one of the health insurance exchanges available through the Affordable Care Act of 2010. This kind of assistance is not cheap, but will honor the Lord and bless that person leaving.

Staff may require some career counsel in cases where they are struggling with direction or need to make a change in how they earn their livelihood. Providing expenses for some help through organizations like IDAK Group (see appendix A) can be of immeasurable encouragement.

Additionally, help with future placement may be in order, including résumé coaching, networking, and providing references. There are many professional firms designed to help ministers find new opportunities, but they often carry a moderate fee. Your church could help with these costs, too. A list of potential resources to assist with these kinds of issues can be found in appendix A.

Be Kind—Regardless of the reason for the termination, staff deserve to be treated with kindness. They were not only a part of your immediate church family but will also continue as a brother or sister in the church universal. We are called to this:

> Be kind to one another, tenderhearted, forgiving one another, as God in Christ forgave you. (Ephesians 4:32)

You can show kindness:

In timing a termination—While a firing based on a moral failure might suggest a speedier exit, most situations give room for more flexibility. Staff should not hear of their termination just before a holiday or vacation. If you have been communicative throughout, of course, the timing will be easier to determine. Be sensitive to their family circumstances, as well. If they have children in school, it would be caring to time their exit at a semester break, or when summer vacation begins. There will potentially be job considerations of a spouse, as well. Being mindful and sensitive to such circumstances will bless your soon-to-be former staff person and reflect well on your leadership.

In communicating a termination—Having informed your departing staff person, you will want to advise their coworkers, volunteers, and most likely the entire church. In doing so, supervising pastors should avoid "spinning" the story. Forget the euphemisms ("We are releasing pastor x to be free to follow God's leading"). Just tell what can be told, and give the staff and congregation something to help them get their heads around the change. Nature abhors a vacuum, and most church people crave something to fill the void. Roy Oswald, an authority in pastor/congregational relationships, says this about pastors (or staff) who are leaving:

> *Usually, however, they slip off into the night without really saying good-bye, and that can undercut everything they've done up till then. People may question whether the pastor really cared for them at all.* [4]

In keeping with Oswald's wisdom, don't first convey this decision by means of the church app or web newsletter. Even with the convenience of such an approach, it makes the whole experience impersonal. There should first be an announcement up front and face to face with the people affected. And if that seems awkward or dangerous to the leadership, then perhaps the rationale for the decision was not that well considered.

Allowing the staff being let go to resign is another demonstration of kindness. Under most circumstances, this will flow normally from the process. But even in difficult cases, it can give the departing staff member some dignity and control in a time of personal distress and anxiety. Sometimes a staff person is not working out well and should be let go, but it's tricky in terms of the potential hard feelings and conflict that might ensue. This is especially true when that individual has been a part of the church for many years. One pastor muses about how his delicate circumstance was resolved:

> *I had a real strong . . . she was almost like an administrative pastor but she had no ministry experience. She was a librarian who had been in the church, we ended up having her be an administrator when we were selling the building and moving. And she would be my prime example of somebody who talks one way to me and another way to other people, just because her temperament, her personality, when she's talking to power then she's nice, friendly, and gracious, and when she's not, she isn't necessarily. And when you say things to her that are questions she can hear them as criticisms when they're not. I did not ask her to leave, and I did not "fix" her, but she ended up leaving because they needed to just reconfigure the staff and it worked out okay.*

In relating to the one being terminated—After I announced my resignation from a pastorate several years ago, I noticed a strange reaction on the part of one lay leader. Seeing him at a nearby mall he managed, our eyes met—and he purposely did not acknowledge my presence. Perhaps he didn't know what to say, or he figured that I'm a part of the past and no longer worthy of his investment. Obviously this hurt my feelings, as I can remember the incident clearly three decades later.

It may be a bit difficult for you and your staff, but keep talking to the one leaving, ask him or her questions, communicate with him or her, and include him or her in your staff meetings and regular social activities if you feel that is appropriate. True, he or she may not feel comfortable sharing ideas about your ministry's vision or future planning, but being treated like a pariah will only deepen the loss already being experienced.

In celebrating their ministry—Departing staff should be celebrated, if possible. A party should be planned where their contributions are acknowledged, and people who love and appreciate them have an opportunity to verbally thank and affirm them. "Crowd funding" could even be arranged, if appropriate, especially in cases where the financial challenge ahead is acute. The difficulty of some terminations may make a larger public celebration inappropriate, but even then, a private gathering can accomplish a similar expression of love for the one leaving.

From a leadership standpoint, treating exiting staff kindly is huge. The potential for bitterness and discouragement among remaining staff and congregational members rises dramatically when terminations are handled poorly. In the past few years in one church I know of, several staff members have been "released" (that's another euphemism), where the firing was abrupt, without any celebrating of the wonderful contributions these brethren had given, some with years of faithful service. The church has suffered because of this, and many congregants have lost trust in their leaders. Many others have left. Be kind to your staff. May you be able to relate to what this pastor reflects concerning his experience with staff transitions over several years:

> *I don't think anybody who I've helped to move along felt like I was out to get them, or I was unfair.*

Be Reflective—You will glean a lot of information and perspective through any termination process. But it will be important, when the going-away party is over and that staff person has left the building, that you reflect on the experience and apply what you've learned to future staffing decisions, job descriptions, expectations, ministry vision, and other considerations unique to your ministry context. Albert Einstein allegedly said, "Insanity is doing the same thing over and over again and expecting different results." Ministry is challenging enough without missing the chance to make it better through careful reflection. One pastor muses about his experience with staff turnover:

> *The last years have been a little bit difficult in terms of the team here gelling . . . a little bit of a turnover . . . we've had a situation with a business administrator that was pretty difficult and that caused a lot of considerable anxiety in the staff. Changes would be made without announcement, and that lasted for maybe about three years. Then after his resignation we spent a*

whole year studying the idea of moving to an executive pastor. That failed to move . . . we failed to be able to pull that off. One of my staff members wanted that position badly, and so in the process he also was not chosen. So it's been a little hard lately. There have been seasons where I would do it over again (differently).

Regardless of the nature of staff transitions, they present a challenge to everyone in any ministry setting. Treating everyone as we would desire to be treated involves all the above commitments, at the very least. Factoring them in to your handling of staff transitions will only help you and your ministry colleagues thrive.

TAKING INVENTORY

Staff transitions are always challenging, but God is able to meet us and guide us in these times and bring good out of them for both the church and the staff member. This is an important time to learn and reflect on what you are doing well in your supervision of your staff members, and what would be good to learn for the future. Consider which issues would be best to focus on, and work through the relevant questions to make this a positive learning experience and help you support your staff members in this time of transition.

Following the Golden Rule of Staff Transitions

Being Patient

Leader: Are there important steps I have not taken in the process of letting this staff person go? Is there time to go back and cover those bases? How will that be arranged?

With Your Associates: Do you feel this process has been incomplete or unfair in any way? How can I (we) address any questions, considerations, or concerns that have not been covered?

Leader: Have I and other leaders estimated the cost of losing this staff member? Where will the resources come from in the interim?

With Your Associates: Have we adequately addressed the cost this decision incurs for you personally? Are there considerations you would like to bring up that we can discuss at this time? What kind of additional support would be welcome and most helpful to you?

Leader: Have I given the staff member adequate resources and opportunity to work on improving his or her performance?

With Your Associates: In what ways could I be more supportive and resourceful to you during your ministry here? (If termination is decided, this question would be: *In what ways could I have been more supportive*, etc.)

Being Communicative

Leader: Is there a clear understanding of staff job expectations, ministry goals, and vision? How can I find out, and clarify where needed?

With Your Associates: Do you have a clear understanding of what your job entails and what is being expected of you? In what areas do you need clarification and guidance? Are there any particulars that are difficult or frustrating to you? (Again, if staff is being let go, these would be explored: *Have you had a clear . . . ?*)

Leader: Have there been regular performance reviews throughout this staff member's tenure? If not, how can I correct this in the near term?

With Your Associates: Are (were) our performance reviews helpful and timely, in your estimation? How would you approach this aspect of our relationship if you were my supervising pastor and I the associate?

Leader: Do we have a structure in place that invites regular and open communication between supervisors and staff?

With Your Associates: Were there ways in which you felt stifled in being open with me in our professional and personal relationship? What could I have done to make our interactions more transparent and edifying?

Leader: Is there a system of record keeping being used for keeping track of supervisor-staff interactions? Do we keep written records of our all-staff meetings?

Leader: When will we conduct an exit interview with the staff person moving on? What questions are important to ask, and do we have a method of retaining what we learn? Who will lead this interview, and how will we use what is learned?

With Your Associates: Whom would you desire to be part of your exit-interview panel? Are there questions and/or points of discussion you want to suggest for our interview?

Being Honest

Leader: Can we as a staff talk at a deep level about a range of issues that affect our working together as a team? What areas seem to be "off limits," and what can be done to open those doors?

With Your Associates: As you reflect on your time here on staff, have you felt free to explore important issues, ideas, or concerns regarding our ministry together? Were there any "taboo" areas you sensed during your tenure? How would you suggest we begin to open up those forbidden areas in the future?

Leader: Have I worked with my staff person in assessing whether it is time for him or her to make a move? How can I provide a safe environment for such a discussion?

With Your Associates: Was I, as your supervisor, diligent in helping you process your call to this ministry over the time we have spent together? Did (do) you feel safe discussing the question of your fit and future on our ministry team? How could I have made this a safer exercise?

Leader: Am I lacking courage in addressing character or work performance concerns with my staff? What issues need to be confronted, and how will I approach this colleague in dealing with them?

With Your Associates: Do you sense that I was unwilling to tackle character or performance issues with you during your ministry here? Could you share any such issues now, so that we might approach them at this time?

Being Well-Intentioned

Leader: Do I convey to my staff a sense of confidence in, and acceptance of them? If not, what can I do to make this more evident to them?

With Your Associates: Do (did) you feel supported and accepted by me during your time here on this staff? What steps could I have taken to provide more encouragement?

Leader: What am I regularly doing to help my staff grow to be the best they can be in their area of service? (See also chapter 7.)

With Your Associates: Do (did) you receive adequate support and resources to grow in your professional areas of ministry while here on staff? What specific ways could I be/have been more helpful to you in your personal ministry progress?

Leader: Is it possible that I look at my staff as a means to an end and not as individuals who labor with me to honor Christ and build His church? Do I need to apologize to anyone in this regard? How can I address this tendency and make necessary changes in my expectations?

With Your Associates: During your time here, have you felt like a cog in the wheel of our ministry machine, instead of like a valued individual whose particular strengths and gifts were recognized and appreciated? If so, how could we change that working atmosphere?

Being Consistent

Leader: Do we have a staff policy manual, and does everyone have a copy? Have we reviewed it together recently, and has it been updated to reflect current realities?

With Your Associates: Have you been adequately made aware of our staff policies? In the future, how could we be clearer and more instructive in this regard? Are there areas where our policies need updating, and would you be willing to help in this task?

Leader: Is there a clear process for dealing with character issues that may require church discipline? Is it being administered fairly and equitably?

Leader: How is poor job performance handled? Do we have a step-by-step procedure to follow in such cases? Are we being well intentioned in the process?

With Your Associates: Do (did) you feel the procedures we have followed in handling your performance evaluation are fair and reasonable? If not, what would have helped?

Being Generous

Leader: Do I know the financial situation my terminated staff person is facing? Is there a way I can find out some basic details and see how others and I might help?

With Your Associates: Would you share with me the true financial picture you are facing as you leave our staff? Can I bring this to our governing board for consideration and response?

Leader: Are we offering severance in this instance? What is our formula for determining the amount?

Leader: What other support can we offer: career counseling, job search assistance, bridging health insurance coverage, moving costs? Are we following our procedures well?

With Your Associates: As you leave our staff and ministry, what kinds of assistance can we offer in this transition time? Could you provide a list of needs, along with the costs involved for each?

Being Kind

Leader: What is the best timing for termination of this staff member? What is best for the congregation and remaining staff and volunteers?

With Your Associates: From your standpoint, what would be the optimal time frame for you leaving this staff position? What kinds of circumstances are you facing that affect this timing, and how can we accommodate you in this regard?

Leader: What is my plan for announcing this staff person's departure? Who will hear personally from me, and in what order? Have I written down my comments and shared them first with the one leaving?

With Your Associates: Would you please read my comments prepared to announce your leaving of our ministry? Are there any changes or other considerations you would like to suggest? Can we agree on who hears this first, and in what order and from whom subsequent announcements are made to the fellowship?

Leader: Am I being considerate of how I and the other associates are treating this staff person, knowing he or she is leaving? How can I purposefully lead others in showing respect, consideration, and inclusion?

With Your Associates: Will you let us know how we are making your transition awkward and/or painful? Can you share those words or actions that are not supportive—and what would be encouraging and helpful to you?

Leader: What celebrative activities have we planned for this staff member's departure? Who would be best qualified to take the lead on coordinating these?

With Your Associates: We want to celebrate your time and ministry with us. What kind of service or activity would mean the most to you and those you have ministered to and alongside over these years? Are there any special requests you would make concerning inviting outside guests, family, and friends not a part of our fellowship?

Being Reflective

Leader: What have I learned throughout this termination process? Have I written it down?

How will I utilize these reflections in the present and future? What particular changes will I make going forward?

Have I treated all involved in this process with the same care and concern I myself would like to be treated with? In what specific ways have I failed, and how will I plan to do better from now on?

Have I sought the reflections of others involved in this experience? What have I learned from their perspectives?

Chapter Nine

Self-Care as a Ministry Supervisor

Mick Boersma

Kevin and I share something beyond our collegial calling here at the seminary. Combined, we've owned the same VW bug for fifty-one years. My dad bought it for me in 1965, and I sold it to Kevin in 1997. He's been the proud owner since then, and it sits out in the school parking lot, some days next to its replacement, my eighteen-year-old Dodge Dakota pickup.

Beside the fact those old VWs were well built, the robust health and longevity it enjoys is a result of careful, loving, and faithful maintenance over the years. As a farm boy, I learned early that taking care of machinery was job one. Our livelihood depended on the tractors and other equipment working well. Caring for it all was not an option.

As a ministry supervisor, you are a precious and critical part of your congregation and staff. It is essential that you invest in caring for yourself, just as you do for your ministry colleagues. Tending to your own person will engender greater effectiveness as you lead, support, and supervise others. It will also give your staff permission to care for themselves, as your example of healthy practices frees them to enjoy the same.

Our purpose in this chapter is to share some thoughts about self-care from our current research, insights gained from years of interaction with ministry leaders, and our own experience in pastoral ministry. There are many good resources available to help you keep yourself in top shape as a follower of Jesus and leader within your ministry. Several of these are listed in appendix A, and when investigated, will lead you to even more helpful sources and ideas. Like our beloved VW bug, we want you to thrive over the long haul!

There are threats to good ministry health, however. Here are a few we hear about often. I'm sure you can add others to this list.

THREATS TO A HEALTHY MINISTRY LIFE

Fatigue—One of the first things I learned years ago from my seminary professor in counseling class was the effect fatigue has on people. He taught us to look out for it in those we sought to help. Often a good night's sleep will improve attitudes and lead to constructive solutions to people's dilemmas. Ministry is by nature often stressful and exhausting, threatening our sense of excitement and hope in the very work we're called to do. One senior pastor we interviewed cites a comment he heard at a pastor's growth conference led by Archibald Hart, clinical psychologist and dean emeritus of the Graduate School of Psychology, Fuller Seminary:

> Somebody asked Dr. Hart, "What's the best advice you can give us to avoid these kinds of issues (anger, burnout, depression)." And he said, "Get ready," and everybody gets ready to write, he says, "You don't need to write, you can remember this. Get more sleep."

Distraction—This could include reading too much news on the Internet, or too many books on the latest, greatest ministry philosophy and/or method, or simply falling too much in love with the myriad diversions this world offers. Our technology can deliver information on a scale that often confuses and numbs us to the deeper, simpler, and more profound realities of life. And the list of things we're told will give us a renewed zest for living is endless— and mostly unsatisfying.

Routine—It's not very popular to assert this notion, but most of life is about maintenance. The jet planes we fly in our travels are built in a relatively short period of time, compared to the thousands of hours of subsequent upkeep that assure a safe landing at our destination. In ministry, we do a lot of things over and over again—good things—but the routine can drain our creativity and leave us exhausted, uninspired, and sometimes just plain cranky.

Disobedience—Have you discovered yet how tiring disobedience is? Perhaps you don't struggle with this as much as I do, but there are areas in my life where I continue to wrestle with God. I suppose it's somewhat like being at odds with any friend or loved one. The lack of harmony between you and the other person wears on you, blocking that pathway of exuberance that should characterize a loving relationship.

Before we explore a prescription for maintaining a healthy ministry life, it is important to identify a few key prerequisites that form a solid foundation for good living and great ministry.

PREREQUISITES OF A HEALTHY MINISTRY LIFE

Convinced of God's Grace—Early in my pastorate, I asked the Lord to make me a grateful man—a son, husband, father, and friend who lives each day consciously thankful for all the bounty that his God has given him. Sure, there are reasons to be discouraged and even ungrateful, but how can I dwell there when all around me are reminders of His awesome grace? And what a privilege to trust in the only true God, who is trustworthy in love and power. As Jeremiah was inspired to pen:

> Blessed is the man who trusts in the Lord, and whose trust is the Lord. He is like a tree planted by water, that sends out its roots by the stream, and does not fear when heat comes, for its leaves remain green, and it is not anxious in a year of drought, for it does not cease to bear fruit. (17:7–9)

Pastor Lee Eclov, in his delightful book *Pastoral Graces*, begins with these words:

> *Doctors enter the practice of medicine. Lawyers, the practice of law. Pastors enter the practice of grace. Grace is our stock in trade.* [1]

He continues a few pages later:

> *Pastors are in the practice of grace for Jesus' sake. Since shepherding is a God-given assignment, it is too hard for us. . . . Years ago I memorized 2 Corinthians 9:8. I have it framed on my wall. "And God is able to make all grace abound to you, so that in all things at all times, having all that you need, you will abound in every good work."* [2]

I imagine that more than a few of us act as if our security in Christ is up to us. If we work harder, do more stuff, get more involved with the church and community—somehow we'll be in better standing with our Lord and Savior.

To combat this tendency, we must never forget the gospel. It is good news. We are the beneficiaries of God's unmerited and unsought favor, redeemed from lives lost by our Father who "*blessed us in Christ with every spiritual blessing in the heavenly places*" (Ephesians 1:3). Ministers who both know and are personally confident in the grace of God are men and women who live and serve from hearts of gratitude, not bondage or fear. From this solid foundation of God's amazing grace, pastors of all sorts can thrive as leaders and colleagues in the work of ministry.

Secure in Our Identity in Christ—The expectations of others is a powerful wind on the ocean of pastoral ministry. Being able to navigate these waters is absolutely essential. Unfortunately, if you do not have a sense of identity in who you are, those winds will drive you unto the rocks of insecurity. My ministry mentor Wally (see chapter 6) encouraged all of us young pastors with this maxim: "Have nothing to prove." He was saying that if we serve from a strong sense of who we are in Christ, we will thrive in the midst of the dizzying array of people's opinions of who we should be.

Especially in times of failure and/or inability to live up to others' expectations, several of our pastoral friends mention the peace of God they experience when remembering their position in Christ. I can personally testify to the blessing experienced by reading the first two chapters of Ephesians every day during the first months of my pastorate—how it reminded me that I brought nothing into this relationship and can take comfort that the Lord loves me just as I was—and am. My sense of self must come from this truth:

> For we are His workmanship, created in Christ Jesus for good works, which
> God prepared beforehand, that we should walk in them. (Ephesians 2:10)

Our labors flow from the complete and eternal salvation we were given, and are an expression of His expert craftsmanship and provision. Embracing this wonderful reality enables us to supervise and work alongside our colleagues with freedom and joy.

Aware of Our God-Given Mission—Surveys consistently affirm that Christian workers, pastors in particular, need a clear sense of God's call in order to thrive in their ministry lives. Jackson Carroll in his excellent compendium of research on pastoral leadership, *God's Potters* (p. 159), underscores this reality by citing a comment from Eugene Peterson:

> *I've loved being a pastor, almost every minute of it. It's a difficult life because it's a demanding life. But the rewards are enormous—the rewards of being on the front line of seeing the gospel worked out in people's lives. I remain convinced that if you are called to it, being a pastor is the best life there is. But any life can be the best life if you're called to it.*

When we know why we've been put on this earth, that God has called us to pastoral service, the daily challenges of being a servant leader do not overwhelm us. Nor are we easily distracted from our primary mission. Early in Jesus's ministry, he performs the miracle of healing Peter's mother-in-law. Upon raising up many who are sick and casting out demons, news spreads quickly. The disciples are getting excited and see an amazing opportunity developing right before their eyes.

So what does Jesus do? He wanders off into the wilderness at the crack of dawn, leaving the gathering crowd in Capernaum and the disciples puzzled, and perhaps even a slight bit frustrated. Once they find him, his response reveals all—he knows his mission and is following it in obedience to his Father. We read:

*And he said to them, "Let us go on to the next towns, that I may preach there also, for this is why I came out." * (Mark 1:38)

Amid the unfathomable sea of human need, he was able to fulfill his task because he understood the calling his Father had given him.

We all know that ministry is endless, that needs abound in virtually infinite amounts. If we do not have a fairly clear sense of why God has put us on this earth, given us this position of ministry—then the limitless need will drive our life, not the orders of our commander-in-chief. It is important that we discover our spiritual gifts, hear the counsel of those who observe our ministry, and keep our hearts open to the directing of our God. The clarity of our call, identity in Christ, and rest in his grace combine to form a solid basis upon which we can give attention to caring for our life as ministers.

PRESCRIPTION FOR MAINTAINING A HEALTHY MINISTRY LIFE

A man's spirit will endure sickness, but a crushed spirit who can bear? (Proverbs 18:14)

Everyone is vulnerable to having his or her spirit broken by the people he or she is called to love and serve. If you're struggling in your ministry right now, regardless of the reasons, perhaps some advice we've heard over the years, and we ourselves have followed, will lead to renewed and sustainable health. This is far from a complete list, but hopefully the ideas we share will both encourage you and give rise to other ways you can tend to your well-being (table 9.1).

Table 9.1.   Prescription for Maintaining a Healthy Ministry Life

Stay in touch with your mentors and close friends

Cherish your loved ones

Remind yourself that hardship is part of ministry

Retain professional experts

Develop and sustain relationships outside of ministry

Maintain balance in living

Commune with God

Keep learning

Be open to a change

Stay in touch with your mentors and close friends—Much support is realized by just having someone you know and respect *hear* your struggles. Any
answers they might suggest are usually less important than knowing they
care and will pray for you. Several of our students and seasoned pastors have
shared that these persons must be safe harbors (people who are not personally involved in our ministry and pose no conflict of interest in its regard).
Mentors who have experienced similar problems, who have "been there," are
cited as most helpful overall.

Ministries like Standing Stone (see appendix A, chapter 6 section) are
being established throughout many networks and denominations in order to
provide personal support for ministry workers. Member care initiatives have
been developed for those serving overseas in myriad cultural settings. At our
own seminary, my wife and I launched a venue for ongoing support for our
alumni over twenty-five years ago. If your alma mater has such resources, be
sure to take full advantage of them.

And one more thing in this regard—embrace and enjoy those deeper
friendships you have nurtured over the years. They may not be a part of your
immediate setting but are a precious gift from God. They've known you a
long time most likely, and love you unconditionally. At my age, I have a
number of such friends. We love each other's company, even if it is on a
social network most of the time. We joke that when we're all retired (when-
ever that is) we'll plant a church together. Could the world endure it!

Cherish your loved ones—Whether married or not, with children or not,
God has given you what I call your "first sheep"—those special people who
are a part of your immediate family. As you support your staff members in
this regard, so must you focus on your own household. What more strategic
investment could you make in guarding the well-being of your life and ministry?

When my wife and I left our church in Washington, our congregants kept
dropping by to say good-bye. They were so supportive and grateful for the
years we spent together. Among all the things they were most grateful for,
the example of our family life was first among them. Personally, I was
hoping it would be my preaching, but alas, it was not. Seeing us live as a
family—that was what made the deepest impression. By God's grace, my
wife and I invested heavily in our marriage and children, making sure the
home front was strong and growing. The effectiveness of following this
prescription was borne out in those good-byes.

That congregation was also our family—cherished loved ones—and leaving them was hard. Our daughters had scores of surrogate grandmothers,
grandpas, aunts, uncles, and siblings. We were leaving our spiritual family.
My wife and I were so blessed to receive the love of this fellowship over
those years. Our personal and family health was protected and bettered by
this amazing community of saints.

Remind yourself that hardship is part of ministry—Suffering is a part of walking in Christ. One ministry colleague affirmed that accepting this helps him to see the bigger picture, and that he'll get through the storm. He may be disappointed in people, but not God, and takes comfort in remembering one of his seminary professors telling him that when one is doing real ministry, persecution will come.

In a recent conversation with a good friend, we chuckled together about how our aging bodies are reminding us of our mortality. We now respond to the question, "So, how are you doing?" with this: "Today, I'm doing great—tomorrow is another day." It is healthy for us to recognize that sickness and disability are a normal part of living, so that when physical challenges come, we're not so overwhelmed or surprised at their occurrence. It's good for ministers to keep a realistic view of ministry, as well. Like my friend and me, one can even laugh about the inconveniences of life itself.

Retain professional experts—Ministry life is complicated enough without having to be an expert in every life-related discipline. This is why I have for many years retained professional experts for support in several areas of daily living. My wife and I have an attorney, a brother in Christ, who cares for legal matters such as wills, trusts, and any other circumstances that might require legal counsel.

As well, we have a good friend who is a certified public accountant. And he knows the nuances of clergy tax law, having himself served in a para church organization for a number of years. For a very affordable fee, he does our taxes and stands ready to give us sage advice throughout the year. And while we are focused on finance, I would mention we also are blessed with a young brother in Christ who excels as our financial advisor.

Also, one of my colleagues in the Department of Christian Ministry & Leadership is a licensed counselor. I like to joke that there's always some free therapy down the hall. But as a pastor some years ago, I enjoyed the ministry of a Christian counselor in a nearby city. He helped me through a few dark valleys for which I am so grateful.

Last, make sure you get a yearly physical (wellness check). If at all possible, stick with one physician for the long term. He or she will get to know you and your medical history and be able to note changes in your overall health. My doctor, whom I've been seeing for some years now, has caught a number of issues that could have become real problems. And when he notes a significant change in my vital statistics, he's quick to inquire about my work, stresses, and family circumstances, any of which might need some attention.

Develop and sustain relationships outside of ministry—Along with mentors and close friends, it is important to socially reach outside the parameters of your life as a minister. Pastors live and breathe ministry. We are what we do. Many find it of great help to build and maintain connections with people whose lives are quite different from theirs. It is both refreshing and humbling to realize the journey other people are taking in this life, and many of us can relate to how having friends and acquaintances in the so-called secular arena provide perspective and balance in times when our world seems to be closing in around us.

In our small community in the Northwest there were many business people I had the privilege to meet. Some became friends in time and proved to be great sources of encouragement, wisdom, and the occasional hilarious round of golf (we were not that talented). A week before we moved away, I walked down Main Street and said good-bye to several of the shopkeepers. While not all were part of our church, or any church, they blessed my heart by sharing their good wishes and even prayers for a bright future. If you're like me, it's easy to let ministry capture all of your time, energy, and resources. Hanging out with those who are not part of your congregation can be a true blessing. And in my case, a few of those eventually ended up trusting Christ and becoming a part of our faith community.

Maintain balance in living—Maintaining balance in life is crucial for long-term pastoral health and will help keep us from getting overwhelmed. Developing hobbies, shooting hoops with buddies, playing with our kids, taking vacations, and keeping a day of Sabbath rest are ideas often mentioned during our discussions with ministers.

Speaking of basketball, if you're like me and have lower-back problems, there are safer alternatives. If possible, a gym membership can be beneficial, if you actually go there and use it, of course. Walking, swimming, gardening, hiking, playing in the park—any kind of physical activity we can manage—is good for our overall health and welfare. Kevin and I live close to our university and find walking or biking to work excellent means of getting to work while assuring regular exercise. Do what works for you in your circumstances and stage of life.

Getting away for some rest is always a good idea. While you may not be able to wander off to some fantasy island, you might consider taking a couple of nights away to get your batteries charged. One of our administrative assistants here recently went off to San Diego for a couple of days. She and her husband got free tickets to Sea World, and played a round of golf on their way back. Some gas and food money, and she returned to the office with a renewed zest and inspiration for the work. Small getaways like this are incredibly energizing.

An associate pastor recalls a time when she struggled with an unhealthy tendency in regard to vacations and time off:

> *About seven years ago I realized I was way out of balance, because I hadn't taken vacation time, and I hadn't set aside time on my Fridays, which are my days off, for doing things that recharge and refuel me. So for vacation, I take a*

minimum of two full weeks off a year. I can't just piece it together with a day here and a day there. It takes me three days to unwind.

Commune with God—There is nothing quite as comforting as bringing the struggles of our life to a loving and powerful heavenly Father. After sharing the challenges facing many of our ministry colleagues throughout our research, Kevin and I enjoy a time of lifting one another's burdens up before the Lord in prayer. As James 5:13–16 encourages us, *"Is anyone among you suffering? Let him pray".* . . . knowing that . . . *"The prayer of a righteous person has great power as it is working."*

When we ask our alumni what keeps them going and motivated in the work, many tell us that along with prayer, daily Bible reading is a key. Staying in the Word of God is always good for our spiritual health. And we'd recommend particularly the Psalms, in that the writers are honest in describing their lives and circumstances. Life in its most challenging times is being met head-on and dealt with openly before God.

Also, there are quiet times, retreats, sitting in silence—spiritual disciplines. As mentioned above, the distractions and noise of our world and work can wear us down and drain us of inspiration. Who is more inspiring than the Creator? Who can restore our hope and show us the way ahead better than God our Father? My routine as a pastor was to start the day reading the Word and letting God speak to my heart. I did not think "sermon preparation," and worked hard at putting the day's schedule out of my mind. It was just He and I. Those were such refreshing times, and still are.

Listen to how one children's ministry supervisor experiences her communion with God:

> *We're allowed to take a solo day once a month where we spend time with Jesus. I had one on Monday, and spent four hours doing a Bible study and another couple hours doing a prayer walk. And in protecting my day off, I do as much as I can leading up to Friday so that on Friday I'm not answering e-mails all day, and I'm not meeting with volunteers, and I'm not constantly picking up the slack. It's better for me to work extra and stay later, and have a full day off on Friday. So it's really a discipline for myself to do that, because otherwise I would be burned out right now. I don't know how somebody could stay in it.*

Keep learning—I used to think that once my degrees were earned, I would just use that information in the ensuing years of ministry. Now I know better. Formal education is basically an introduction to a life of learning. And whether one has the privilege of higher education or not, they soon realize there is much more to explore in this amazing world than they could imagine.

When discovering new knowledge, you don't have to focus on your particular discipline exclusively. Throughout my years in ministry, I've enjoyed investigating the field of archaeology and am making my way through several reports written by scholars and "diggers" in the Middle East. And you don't have to enter a formal degree program, either. As mentioned in the preceding chapters, there are many opportunities to learn at conferences, both those that relate to your particular field, and others that are just good for rounding out your education.

Be open to a change—It is quite possible that having considered your ministry situation and spiritual health, remaining where you are could be toxic to your soul. We've seen it happen and question the wisdom of someone staying in a setting where the joy of the Lord is slowly being extinguished. Stepping out of a position should never come easy, but sometimes it is the right move for you, your loved ones, and your ministry future.

In chapter 8 we addressed the issue of helping your staff discern their career path, including the process of helping them move on, if such is deemed necessary or appropriate. Those same resources are there for you as well and can help you assess the path your ministry life should take.

After eleven years of pastoring our church, the dream of teaching in a Christian university was rekindled in my mind and heart. Thirty-one years ago my wife and I, along with our daughters, loaded up our belongings and made our way to southern California. All I can say is—the Lord is faithful. These years have been an inspiration to our children and us—a whole new chapter of amazing opportunities and experiences.

TAKING INVENTORY

Paying attention to your own health and well-being has great benefits for you, your church, and those who work closely with you. Consider these questions and determine what might be some important changes to make to build your well-being. If you are married, consider discussing these with your spouse. He or she may see some issues or concerns that you are not seeing well. Trust that God can use him or her for your care and growth.

Threats to a Healthy Ministry Life

1. ***Fatigue***—How many hours of sleep do I usually get each night? Are there particular times when I'm really tired, and do I know what may cause this? Am I trying to do too much at the job and/or during my off hours?
2. ***Distraction***—Has the amount of time I spend on social media gotten out of hand? What other activities occupy too much of my time? Which of these could I eliminate or reduce?

3. *Routine*—What aspects of my work do I find particularly numbing, and why? How long has it been since I (and my family) have done something not related to my ministry?

4. *Disobedience*—Are there practices or attitudes in my personal life that need to be confessed to the Lord? Are there people I need to go to for forgiveness, or to restore our relationship?

Prerequisites of a Healthy Ministry Life

1. *Convinced of God's grace*—Do I have a sense of inner peace before the Lord? What are the signs in my life that He is gracious—what am I thankful for? Am I trying to gain His approval by working extra hard? Is my performance in ministry the basis of my feeling accepted by God? If so, where did this come from, and how does God's grace impact this unhealthy attitude?

2. *Secure in my identity in Christ*—When is the last time I spent personal time reading through Paul's letters, especially Ephesians? Have I reviewed the beauty and power of the gospel lately? Is my sense of identity wrapped up in my gifts and abilities? Do I revel in the knowledge I am a child of God, crafted by him for good works?

3. *Aware of my God-given mission*—What made me excited about being in ministry in the first place? How has my calling changed over the years? When is the last time I worked through my calling with God and my mentor and/or advisor? What might be causing my sense of calling to wane, if it is?

Prescription for Maintaining a Healthy Ministry Life

1. *Stay in touch with mentors and close friends*—When is the last time I connected with those I consider my mentors? What is necessary for me to set up an appointment to talk and catch up? Have I spent time with my close friends in the last few months? Do I keep these relationships a priority, and how will I make sure they remain so?

2. *Cherish my loved ones*—Am I treating my immediate family as my "first sheep"? If not, why not? What steps can I take to demonstrate that they are a priority and a treasure to me? In what ways can I reflect this dedication to my staff and congregation, as well?

3. *Remind myself that hardship is a part of ministry*—Do I accept the reality of hardship as a part of ministry life? What particular struggles are most difficult for me, and why? Do I have someone to go to (mentor, friend, even my spouse) to share these struggles with and keep them in perspective?

4. ***Retain professional experts***—Do I have a select group of professional counselors to help me handle any legal, financial, psychological, or medical issues? If not, are there people I trust who could help me identify individuals or firms to provide such support?

5. ***Develop and sustain relationships outside of ministry***—Am I living exclusively in my ministry world, not connected to the community in which I live? What organizations, clubs, sports clubs, or other community-based activities could I investigate as pathways into the world outside my bubble? What entertainments, events, or community services could provide both time with my family and relationship-building opportunities with my neighbors?

6. ***Maintain balance in life***—What kind of "short break" opportunities are available in my geographic area? Where will I get away and have some down time in the next thirty days? Am I fully utilizing my days off? What is keeping me from getting a complete break from my responsibilities when taking them? Am I handling social media, or is it handling me?

7. ***Commune with God***—When and where will I purposefully spend time alone with God? What will it take for me to daily connect with him? In my reading, what is my plan? What spiritual disciplines would work best for me—solitude, praying through the Scriptures, silence, fasting, worship, reflection, journaling?

8. ***Keep learning***—Have I kept growing in knowledge and perspective concerning my field of ministry work? If not, why not? Are there educational opportunities available that might inspire me to grow? (See chapter 7.) Is there a field of knowledge that intrigues me outside my ministry profession? How can I pursue the enjoyment of exploring that world?

9. ***Be open to a change***—Am I sensing that it's time to consider a move? What are my reasons? Have I considered the many factors involved in making such a decision? (as itemized in *Moving On Moving Forward; A Guide for Pastors in Transition*—see appendix A, chapter 8 section) Have I consulted with my trusted mentors, friends, and ministry colleagues concerning this possibility?

Appendix A

Resources for Supervising Pastors

We've put together a list of some helpful resources on a wide range of issues addressed in the chapters of this book. With each resource we've added some comments about what it is about and how it may be of help to you. Identify those issues that may be most beneficial for you to address as a supervisor, and keep reading and reflecting on how you might grow and strengthen your supervision and support of your staff.

CHAPTER 1: INTRODUCTION: FOUNDATIONS FOR SUPERVISING AND SUPPORTING ASSOCIATE STAFF

Susan Beaumont and Gil Rendle, *When Moses Meets Aaron: Staffing and Supervision in Large Congregations*, Rowman & Littlefield, 2007. Excellent work on some basic supervision issues, particularly strong on legal issues.

William R. DeLong (Ed.), *Courageous Conversations: The Teaching and Learning of Pastoral Supervision,* UPA, 2009. Though written with a clinical pastoral education focus, there is much here that is helpful for a supervisor working with associate staff members. Addresses issues of working with interns, pastoral identity, skill development, ethics, gender and sexuality, and spiritual formation.

Abigail Johnson, *Shaping Spiritual Leaders: Supervision and Formation in Congregations*, Rowman & Littlefield, 2007. Written with a focus on seminary field education students and interns, many of the issues and principles discussed fit well with general supervision of others in ministry. Helpful sections on conflict management, power and authority, giving feedback, and mutual growth.

Jane Leach and Michael Paterson, *Pastoral Supervision: A Handbook* (2nd ed.), Hymns Ancient & Modern, 2015. A British book addressing the process of supervision of others in ministry. It provides a helpful orientation to the focus of supervision for the sake of the growth and development of the supervisee. Offers much for reflection on the supervisory relationship, with some foundational theological perspectives on the work of supervision. Most helpful for the "developmental" work of supervising others.

Kenneth Pohly, *Transforming the Rough Places: The Ministry of Supervision* (2nd ed.), Providence House Publishers, 2001. Pohly provides a historical perspective on the supervision of others in ministry, and a model for supervision. Though written with a focus on interns and mentoring relationships, it offers helpful ideas for the developmental aspects of supervising staff members.

William T. Pyle, *Experiencing Ministry Supervision*, B&H Academic, 1994. Written for an internship situation, provides many helpful practices for working with a newer, less experienced associate staff member.

Reflective Practice: Formation and Supervision in Ministry, Journals.sfu.ca. An open access journal in the area of ministry supervision. Back issues are available to review, providing insights and ideas on a variety of supervision topics.

Jessica Rose and Michael Paterson (Eds.), *Enriching Ministry: Pastoral Supervision in Practice*, SCM Press, 2014. A UK-context book on ministerial formation. Good sections on theological foundations for ministry supervision, and promoting reflective practice.

CHAPTER 2: FORMING AND LEADING THE MINISTRY TEAM

Books on Teams and Teamwork

W. Gibb Dyer, Jeffrey H. Dyer, and William G. Dyer, *Team Building: Proven Strategies for Improving Team Performance* (5th ed.), Jossey-Bass, 2013. A classic text on team development. Good sections on conflict resolution, cross-cultural teamwork, and ways of developing strong teamwork over time.

Ron R. Katzenbach and Douglas K. Smith, *The Wisdom of Teams*, Harvard Business Press, 1992. Excellent introduction to issues of "real teams" vs. "work groups" and leadership practices that fit each situation best.

Ron R. Katzenbach and Douglas K. Smith, *The Discipline of Teams*, John Wiley & Sons, 2001. Follow-up to their earlier work, with more practical advice on the kinds of practices that help teams and other kinds of workgroups continue to function effectively over time.

Frank LaFasto and Carl Larson, *When Teams Work Best*, Sage, 2001. Follow-up to their earlier book (1989), providing additional insights to leadership practices that help teams be effective.

Carl Larson and Frank LaFasto, *Teamwork: What Must Go Right, What Can Go Wrong*, Sage, 1989. Classic work of original research on key factors for team effectiveness. Excellent orientation to eight key aspects of team practices, with insights for those who lead.

Patrick Lencioni, *The Five Dysfunctions of a Team: A Leadership Fable*, Jossey-Bass, 2002. A helpful look at common stresses and dysfunctions that can develop in teams over time, and ways to address them to enhance team effectiveness.

Books on Teams in Ministry

William J. Carter, *Team Spirituality: A Guide for Staff and Church*, Abingdon Press, 1997. A helpful book on common staff ailments and diagnostic tools to help draw out feedback for discussion. Addresses the spiritual base of church leadership, particularly the leadership of others on staff. Excellent resource for staff development.

George Cladis, *Leading the Team-Based Church*, Jossey-Bass, 1999. Strong on developing collaboration in ministry, rooted in a strong Trinitarian theology. Good material on developing a team covenant, positive culture, trust, and a learning and growing environment.

Ryan T. Hartwig and Warren Bird, *Teams That Thrive: Five Disciplines of Collaborative Church Leadership*, IVP Books, 2015. Provides diagnostic tools to assess how well your team is thriving, and five disciplines that help people work well together on ministry teams. Written with a focus on leadership behaviors that help others thrive in collaborative work.

M. Anne Burnette Hook and Shirley F. Clement, *Staying Focused: Building Ministry Teams for Christian Formation*, Discipleship Resources, 2002. Though written with a focus on church committees and ministry teams with lay leaders, there are many helpful perspectives and practices that also fit leading and developing a pastoral ministry team. Addresses aspects of group prayer, Scripture study, and worship in the midst of ministry together.

John C. Maxwell, *The 17 Indisputable Laws of Teamwork: Embrace Them and Empower Your Team*, Thomas Nelson, 2001. Maxwell addresses a range of principles and practices for developing an effective team. While some may not fit well in the ministry context, others do, and can stimulate some creative thinking for how to strengthen your ministry team.

Larry Osborne, *Sticky Teams: Keeping Your Leadership Team and Staff on the Same Page*, Zondervan, 2010. Written for a broader church ministry focus, there are many helpful practices for building unity of vision and collaboration, what team leaders need to do, and how to build strong work relationships both within the staff and with other groups of leaders in the church (e.g., boards).

Stanley E. Ott, *Transform Your Church with Ministry Teams*, Eerdmans, 2004. Written with a lay leadership orientation, the book has many helpful practices for building team fellowship and fostering healthy communication that can fit the church staff team as well.

John T. Trent, Rodney Cox, and Eric Tooker, *Leading from Your Strengths: Building Close-Knit Ministry Teams*, Broadman & Holman, 2004. Examines four key transitions that groups must go through to become an effective ministry team (i.e., problems and challenges, people and information, pace and change, rules and procedures). Addresses the use of the "Strengths Finder" materials to better understand your leadership style and the strengths of team members so you can work better together.

CHAPTER 3: TIME TOGETHER, PART I: CONSTRUCTIVE REGULAR TEAM MEETINGS

Paul Axtell, *Meetings Matter: 8 Powerful Strategies for Remarkable Conversations*, Jackson Creek Press, 2015. Award-winning book on designing meetings for results, leading people through the agenda in ways that help them feel heard, move projects forward, and build relationships in the process.

Ingrid Bens, *Facilitating with Ease! Core Skills for Facilitators, Team Leaders and Members, Managers, Consultants, and Trainers* (3rd ed.), Jossey-Bass, 2012. Addresses how to become a stronger group facilitator, run productive meetings, and help others on the team do so as well.

Dianna Booher, *Leading Effective Meetings: 72 Tips to Save Time, Improve Teamwork, and Make Better Decisions*, Booher Research Institute, 2012. A very short e-book of helpful ideas for managing team meetings, drawing out participation, avoiding issues that can derail the group, and leading discussions.

Anne M. Bosarge, *Ministry Meeting Starters: Fun, Team-Building Meeting Starters to Refocus, Refresh, and Renew your Passion for Ministry*, CreateSpace Independent Publishing Platform, 2014. Useful activities to cast ministry vision and develop a healthy culture in your ministry team. One of the few resources of its kind written for ministry team leaders.

Harvard Business Review, *Running Meetings* (Harvard Business Review 20 Minute Manager Series), Harvard Business Review Press, 2014. Practical advice on creating agendas, making sure people are drawn out and heard, avoiding conflict situations, and follow up on group decisions.

Patrick Lencioni, *Death by Meeting: A Leadership Fable*, Jossey-Bass, 2004. Addresses some of the common problems that can develop in groups that meet on a regular basis. Provides a helpful guide for regular weekly meetings where decisions must be made together.

Glenn M. Parker, *Effective Meetings: 20 Sure-Fire Tools* (Vol. II, The Parker Team Series), HRD Press, 2009. Very practical, this book focuses on key practices to ensure that the goals of a meeting are achieved: problem solving, decision making, plan developing, question answering, and more.

Al Pittampalli, *Read This Before Our Next Meeting: How We Can Get More Done*, Portfolio, 2015. This book lays out eight simple principles for making meetings shorter and more productive. While some may not be as critical in the church staff context, this is still a very helpful look at ways to make meeting time more productive, wasting less of everyone's time.

Jessica Pryce-Jones and Julia Lindsay, *Running Great Meetings and Workshops for Dummies*, For Dummies, 2014. Very practical look at a range of foundational practices and details that can make meetings and training events more beneficial for all who participate. From planning to leading, the book addresses common mistakes and how to avoid them.

CHAPTER 4: TIME TOGETHER, PART II: PROFITABLE OCCASIONAL TEAM GATHERINGS AND ONE-ON-ONES

Bill Birnbaum, *Preparing for Your Strategic Planning Meetings: Ten Steps to Success*, Douglas Mountain Publishing, 2014. How to use preplanning surveys to prepare well for group strategic planning. Helps prepare team members to participate well in the process. Addresses common logistical issues for making the meeting a success.

Bill Birnbaum, *Facilitating Strategic Planning Meetings: A Strategy Consultant's Guide*, Douglas Mountain Publishing, 2016. Ways to prepare team members to focus on the key issues to be addresses in strategic planning, lead highly opinionated people through the discussion toward a beneficial conclusion, and work toward implementation of the plan.

Anne M. Bosarge, *Refresh, Revive, Renew: Prayer Retreats for Church Staff*, CreateSpace Independent Publishing Platform, 2014. Very helpful book on monthly prayer retreats for the ministry team. Whether you can do them every month or not, the book provides a helpful plan for team spiritual renewal through extended group prayer times.

Dan R. Ebener and Fred L. Smith, *Strategic Planning: An Interactive Process for Leaders*, Paulist Press, 2015. Offers a step-by-step process for effective strategic-planning meetings. Addresses planning and preparing for the group time, prioritizing needs, developing healthy communication in the group, and accountability for implementation of group decisions.

John C. Endres and Elizabeth Liebert, *A Retreat with the Psalms: Resources for Personal and Communal Prayer*, Paulist Press, 2001. A resource book for using the psalms as a focus for prayer, including praying together with others (like your ministry team). A creative book that will provide you with new ways of reflecting on and praying the psalms together.

Nancy Ferguson and Kevin T. Witt, *The Retreat Leader's Manual: A Complete Guide to Organizing Meaningful Christian Retreats*, Discipleship Resources, 2006. Highly practical book for planning and leading retreats. Very helpful for those who plan and lead church staff retreats.

Rachel Gilmore, *Complete Leader's Guide to Christian Retreats*, Judson Press, 2009. Like the book above, this is a very practical book on planning and leading retreats. It can help you think through the purposes of your retreat and how to craft it to minimize distractions.

Merianne Liteman, Sheila Campbell, and Jeffrey Liteman, *Retreats That Work: Everything You Need to Know about Planning and Leading Great Offsites* (Expanded Edition), Pfeiffer, 2016. Provides a wide range of group-activity ideas for staff retreats that focus on ministry development and decisions.

Aubrey Malphurs, *Advanced Strategic Planning: A 21st-Century Model for Church and Ministry Leaders* (3rd ed.), Baker Books, 2013. A strategic-planning book written for ministry leaders. Very helpful for understanding ways to prepare well for the group meeting, lead the group through the meeting well, examine key foundations for the group's future ministry, and follow up.

Gill Rendle and Alice Mann, *Holy Conversations: Strategic Planning as a Spiritual Practice for Congregations*, Rowman & Littlefield, 2003. Explores strategic planning in the congregational context, not just among staff members. A helpful toolbox of practices and procedures to facilitate the group process in strategic planning.

J. Randolph Turpin Jr., *Shared Discernment: A Workbook for Ministry Planning Teams*, CreateSpace Independent Publishing Platform, 2011. Provides a spiritual reflection process for groups to discern God's guidance in the strategic-planning process. Workbook format included to help in the preparation for a "summit meeting" kind of retreat, experiencing it together, and following up on it once it is over.

CHAPTER 5: FACILITATING AND SUPPORTING THE MINISTRY OF YOUR ASSOCIATE STAFF

Cameron L. Morrissey, *The 7 Deadly Sins of Leadership: And How to Overcome Them in Yourself and Others*, CreateSpace Independent Publishing Platform, 2014. Identifies how we fall into the trap of micromanaging others, and how to work our way out of that trap when we realize we are in it. Addresses a range of other helpful leadership issues, and offers practical ways to deal with the leadership sins we commit.

Adam Tinsdale, *Outdo One Another: Fostering Honor among Pastoral Colleagues* (Strengthen the Church Series, Book 3), Doulos Resources, 2015. How to cultivate mutual respect and encouragement in the midst of ministry together. A short book, but one of the few written on this topic for church staff settings.

CHAPTER 6: SUPPORTING STAFF PERSONALLY

Henry Blackaby and Richard Blackaby, *Called to be God's Leader: Lessons from the Life of Joshua*, Thomas Nelson, 2003. Bestselling author and trusted Bible teacher Henry Blackaby, along with his son Richard, president of Canadian Baptist Seminary, demonstrates through the life of Joshua how God prepares those He chooses for spiritual leadership. Purpose, Obedience, Faith, Character, and Influence are among the themes that are included in this book; key truths are emphasized at the end of each chapter.

Bill Hybels, *Leadership Axioms: Powerful Leadership Proverbs*, Zondervan, 2008. Good leaders can pinpoint the rationale for their actions and decisions with the ease of reciting their home address. In *Axioms*, author Bill Hybels divulges the God-given convictions that have dictated his leadership strategy for more than three decades as senior pastor of Willow Creek Community Church.

Kevin E. Lawson and Mick Boersma, *Associate Staff Ministry: Thriving Personally, Professionally, and Relationally*, Rowman & Littlefield, 2014. While mainly focused on helping associate staff members thrive, the book also contains a chapter for supervising pastors, and another for church boards, on how to help their staff members thrive. Could be a good book to read and discuss together.

Peter Scazzero, *Emotionally Healthy Spirituality*, Zondervan, 2014. In this bestselling book, the author outlines his journey and the signs of emotionally unhealthy spirituality. Then he provides seven biblical, reality-tested ways to break through to the revolutionary life Christ meant for you.

Peter Scazzero, *The Emotionally Healthy Leader*, Zondervan, 2015. Bestselling author Peter Scazzero shows leaders how to develop a deep inner life with Christ, examining its profound implications for surviving stress, planning and decision making, building teams, creating healthy culture, influencing others, and much more.

Standing Stone Ministry, www.standingstoneministry.org. Standing Stone Ministry's threefold mission to (1) care for pastoral couples at risk of leaving the ministry; (2) educate church boards and members on the challenges and needs of their pastoral teams and how they can be more effective in caring for them; and (3) establish mentoring relationships between experienced pastors and graduating students going into full-time vocational ministry.

Rick Warren, *The Purpose Driven Life*, Zondervan, 2002, 2011, 2012. This book has been translated into eighty-five different languages and has become the "best selling non-fiction hardback book in history" according to *Publisher's Weekly*, all because of the Christ-centered approach the book takes to answering life's most fundamental question: What on earth am I here for?

Lance Witt, *Replenish*, Baker Books, 2011. Every leader functions on two stages—the front stage or public world, and the back stage or private world. One cannot lead successfully frontstage when one is completely depleted backstage. *Replenish* helps leaders focus on the back stage, the interior life, in order to remain spiritually healthy.

CHAPTER 7: STAFF REVIEW AND DEVELOPMENT

Eric Barton, "Why You Don't Give Praise in Japan," August 23, 2016, BBC News, http://www.bbc.com/capital/story/20160822-why-you-dont-give-praise-in-japan.

The Effective Church Group, EffectiveChurch.com. Founded by Bill Easum in the 1980s, this resource features articles and blogs by noted experts on a wide range of subjects aimed at helping churches be faithful and effective in present times.

FreeChurchForms.com, see this page on staff reviews: http://www.freechurchforms.com/employee-evaluation-template.html. While this site does sell products for church use, it includes a wide array of free resources, including this article highlighting staff reviews. Several evaluation forms (including staff self-evaluation) are available in the page above as free downloads.

Free PDF form, "What Items to Include in a Church Staff Evaluation," http://s3.amazonaws.com/texasbaptists/connections/Church-Staff-Evaluation-Form.pdf. The Baptist General Conference of Texas Baptists has provided this form through Amazon Web Services Simple Cloud Storage Service, and it is available as a free download at the address above. It includes several key questions for the staff person, and a scaled evaluation instrument for the supervisor(s).

Patrick Lencioni, *The Five Dysfunctions of a Team*, Jossey-Bass, 2002. Lencioni tells a tale in this book, unpacking dysfunctions that cripple teams,

including number 4 "Avoidance of Accountability." Included is a team assessment instrument, along with a strategy for overcoming the dysfunctions.

Patrick Lencioni, *The Advantage*, Jossey-Bass, 2012. This book focuses on
organizational health, presenting a four-disciplines model that is designed to
assist any organization, including church and para church ministries, thrive in
their mission.

Thom S. Rainer Blog, "Growing Healthy Churches. Together," ThomRain-
er.com. This site provides a doorway into many resources related to the
subject of this chapter and most others in this research. Thom Rainer is the
president and CEO of LifeWay Christian Resources.

Tim Spivey.com, see article URL on staff reviews: http://timspivey.com/a-
step-by-step-church-staff-review-guide/. Tim is a lead planter of New Vin-
tage Church in Escondido, California. He is a regular contributor to *Church
Executive*, and *ChurchLeaders.com*. His blogs include helpful essays and
resources on a wide range of church-related issues. This blog article includes
a free download of an excellent staff review form that can be used by supervisors and other leaders who participate in regular staff evaluations.

CHAPTER 8: LETTING GO—STAFF TRANSITIONS

Michael Anthony and Mick Boersma, *Moving On Moving Forward; A Guide
for Pastors in Transition*, Zondervan, 2007. Whether you are searching for
your first position or are a seasoned veteran wrestling with if, when, and how
to move on, *Moving On Moving Forward* will help you navigate the ins and
outs of the ministry employment maze. Topics covered include dealing with
search committees, writing a letter of resignation, preparing a résumé, nego-
tiating compensation, and more. Includes charts and worksheets.

John R. Cionca, *Before You Move*, Kregel, 2004. From discerning one's
personal strengths to discovering job opportunities, from researching to interviewing, from the Holy Spirit's guidance to a congregation's call—all aspects of vocational Christian service and ministry transitions are covered in
this resource.

"Despite Stresses, Few Pastors Give Up on Ministry," www.lifeway.com.
Article URL: http://lifewayresearch.com/2015/09/01/despite-stresses-few-
pastors-give-up-on-ministry/. This article displays the highly reliable research characteristic of LifeWay concerning the dropout rate of pastors
across the United States, and includes helpful perspective on related issues.

Besides LifeWay Research, other reliable research organizations include: Pew Research Center, Gallup, Barna Group, General Social Survey, The Heritage Foundation, and Hoover Institution. Ed Stetzer at LifeWay also added a few specific religious ones like ARIS (American Religious Identification Survey), the ARDA (The Association of Religion Data Archives), and Baylor Religion Survey. From *VitalMagazine.com*, "How to Navigate the Headlines," Tally Whitehead, December 4, 2015.

Robert W. Dingman, *In Search of a Leader*, Dingman Press, 1994. This book is a practical handbook for search committees, and contains everything needed for a well-run search process. Authored by a highly regarded professional search expert, it is full of excellent ideas, strategies, and resources.

"Five Resources for Pastors in Transition," www.lifeway.com. Article URL: http://www.lifeway.com/pastors/2015/09/02/five-resources-for-pastors-in-transition/. Five key articles include résumé help, deciding about a move, and interviewing tips written by well-known and respected authorities in the ministry field.

Cal Habig, www.valuedrivenleaders.com. Cal Habig is an ICF-certified professional coach who helps leaders of small businesses and nonprofit organizations to develop plans and structures that increase their profitability. Cal began his coaching practice in 2009 after thirty years leading several nonprofit organizations and serving on the boards of numerous other organizations. [Taken from website.] He also coaches pastors and served several years as a local church pastor himself.

Richard R. Hammar, JDL, LLM, CPA, *Church Law & Tax*, "Pastor, Church & Law," "Employment Law," www.churchlawandtax.com. A ministry of *Christianity Today*, the mission of CL&T is "keeping your church safe, legal, and financially sound." A yearly subscription is necessary to access this resource.

IDAK Group, IDAKgroup.com. Since its beginning in 1980, IDAK has focused on the assessment of a person's full potential from an organizational and career-planning perspective. The specialty, which IDAK has pioneered and has now become its trademark, is assessing innate natural talents as the key predictor for best job fit. This aptitude specialty is separate from the more commonly measured personality characteristics, work skills, or education or training equivalents. IDAK has become recognized nationally as one of a very select few organizations that recognize natural talents as critical to the question of maximum productivity and mid-career advancement. [Taken from website.]

Bo Lane, *Why Pastors Quit*, CreateSpace Independent Publishing Platform, 2014, www.expastors.com. Whether you've spent your entire career as a pastor or if you have recently thrown in the towel, *Why Pastors Quit* is an easy-to-read book that will encourage you and make you ask the question: What can I do to help change the statistics?

Kevin E. Lawson and Mick Boersma, *Associate Staff Ministry: Thriving Personally, Professionally, and Relationally*, Alban Institute, 2014. Based on updated research and interviews with over six hundred veteran associate staff members from many different denominations, we describe the priorities, attitudes, and practices that can help associate staff members thrive in their ministry roles. We present, explain, and illustrate the four-part Model for Thriving in Associate Staff Ministry, a concrete framework that readers can use to help achieve satisfaction and balance in their own lives.

Warren Lynn, *Exit Interviews When a Church Staff Member Leaves*, 2014, https://www.discipleshomemissions.org/clergy/search-call/downloadable-and-online-ministry-resources/. This is a downloadable article that articulates the uniquenesses of exit interviews in church ministry contexts. A very helpful list of specific exit interview questions is included.

Roberta Chinsky Matuson, *Employee Termination: How to Graciously Let Go of Long-Term Employees*, Monster.com, Employee Termination—Ho#BD8F50. This article gives a helpful and well-reasoned approach to handling both employee evaluations and termination, when necessary.

Dan Reiland, Developing Church Leaders, DanReiland.com, "One Major Principle for Hiring and Firing." Dan is executive pastor at 12Stone Church in Lawrenceville, Georgia. He is best known as a leader with a pastor's heart and coach's instincts, and is described as one of the nation's most innovative church thinkers. His website includes resources on the church, leadership, ministry, spiritual life, staffing, and relationships.

Gil Rendle and Susan Beaumont, *When Moses Meets Aaron: Staffing and Supervision in Large Congregations*, chapter 13, "Dealing with Poor Performance or Terminating Employment," Alban Institute, 2007. These longtime Alban consultants have developed this book to help clergy responsible for several-member staff teams navigate these unknown waters. They have taken the best of human resource practices and immersed them in a congregational context, providing a comprehensive manual for supervising, motivating, and coordinating staff teams.

Slingshot Group, http://slingshotgroup.org/. This company assists churches in finding the right staff, and they help potential candidates in a number of ways, http://slingshotgroup.org/candidates.

CHAPTER 9: SELF-CARE AS A MINISTRY SUPERVISOR

Jackson W. Carroll, *God's Potters: Pastoral Leadership and the Shaping of Congregations*, Eerdmans, 2006. A veteran clergy watcher, Carroll uses data from what is likely the most representative survey of Protestant and Catholic clergy ever undertaken, as well as focus group interviews and congregational responses, to take a hard look at who is doing ministry today, what it involves, and how pastors are faring in leading their congregations.

Lee Eclov, *Pastoral Graces*, Moody Publishers, 2012. This book is required reading for our pastoral ministry students in one of their field education courses. Wisdom from a long career in pastoral ministry is shared throughout.

Bruce Epperly, *A Center in the Cyclone*, Rowman & Littlefield, 2014. This is a resource for integrated personal and professional transformation and healing for pastors, better equipping them to be effective spiritual leaders for the long haul of professional ministry. It was written to deepen Christian leaders' commitments to spiritual growth and self-care practices to ensure healthy and effective ministry over the long haul.

Rochelle Melander and Harold Eppley, *The Spiritual Leader's Guide to Self-Care*, Alban Institute, 2002. This guide gives readers the tools to discern God's intention for their lives and to be faithful to that vision through proper self-care. Included are journal-writing suggestions, personal reflection questions and activities, guidance for sharing the discovery process with another person, an activity for the coming week, and suggested further resources, such as novels, videos, and websites.

Roy M. Oswald, *Clergy Self-Care: Finding a Balance for Effective Ministry*, Rowman & Littlefield, 1991. Nationally known for his work and teaching on clergy development, Oswald integrates research and experience to reveal a path toward health and wholeness. Lots of self-assessment tools, anecdotal references, and self-care strategies are included.

Dan Reiland, Developing Church Leaders, DanReiland.com, "Leaders in Search of Inner Peace"; "The Danger of Desperate Leadership." These two articles provide perspecctve and hope for pastors to enjoy a deeper walk with Christ and more freedom from anxiety in the midst of the pressures of ministry.

Marshall Shelley and Dean Merrill, "The Pastor's Passages," *Leadership Journal* 4 (Fall 1983), 12–19. An interview with Roy Oswald regarding passages and seasons in a pastor's life and how to navigate stresses and changes well in ministry. Addresses the importance of leaving a parish well as part of preparing to enter a new one.

Warren W. Wiersbe and David W. Wiersbe, *10 Power Principles for Christian Service*, Baker Books, 1997, 2010. These two seasoned pastors offer underlying timeless principles that factor into the health and effectiveness of pastoral ministry in any setting.

William Willimon and numerous authors, *The Pastor's Guide to Personal Spiritual Formation,* Beacon Hill Press, 2005. Experienced church leaders, who understand firsthand the importance of maintaining one's own spiritual formation, challenge and inspire pastors to reach new and deeper levels of spiritual vitality and growth. Willimon and other well-known church leaders discuss topics related to spiritual direction, prayer, meditation, Sabbath keeping, and more.

Michael Todd Wilson and Brad Hoffman, *Preventing Ministry Failure,* IVP, 2007. Authors Wilson and Hoffman, senior pastor and licensed counselor respectively, present a personal guidebook for people in ministry to prepare them to withstand common pressures and to flourish in the ministry God has called them to. Lots of wisdom and hands-on exercises are provided.

Appendix B

Overview of the Research Process

Our research efforts behind what is shared in this book consisted of two main parts. First, we carried out an electronic survey with people who had served, or were currently serving, in associate staff roles and asked them to respond to the following four questions:

1. From your experience, past and/or present, as an associate staff member in a church setting: What did your supervising pastor do that helped you take responsibility for your ministry area and grow in your ability to do it well? Please try to give us some examples, and explain why they were helpful to you.
2. From your experience, past and/or present, as an associate staff member in a church setting: What did your supervising pastor do that helped you feel personally supported in the midst of your ministry responsibilities and challenges? Please try to give us some examples, and explain why they were helpful to you.
3. From your experience, past and/or present, as an associate staff member in a church setting: What did your supervising pastor do that hindered, or made more difficult, your taking responsibility for your ministry area and growing in your ability to do it well? Please try to give us an example or two, and explain why this made your work more difficult.
4. From your experience, past and/or present, as an associate staff member in a church setting: What did your supervising pastor do that made you not feel personally supported in the midst of your ministry respon-

sibilities and challenges? Please try to give us an example or two, and explain why this had a negative impact on you.

In the fall of 2015, we sent this survey invitation to over eight hundred recent alumni from Talbot School of Theology, a nondenominational evangelical Protestant seminary in southern California. Our students come from a wide range of denominations, and though many of them serve churches in California after they graduate, they can be found all across the United States and in many other countries. Many of our graduates serve, at least initially, in associate-church-staff roles. Not knowing who may or may not have had this experience, we invited all of these recent alumni to respond to the survey if they had served as associate staff members in a church setting. One hundred and fifty alumni responded and provided reflections on their current or past experiences as associate staff members with their ministry supervisors.

In addition to asking for their responses to these four questions, we also explained that we were looking to interview exemplary ministry supervisors. We invited those who had experienced a particularly good ministry supervisor to e-mail us with that person's name and contact information so we could ask to interview them about their perspectives and practices as a supervisor. About twenty supervisors were identified this way, and in the winter and spring of 2016 we were able to arrange interviews with sixteen of them. In each case, we either met at a restaurant and carried out the interview over lunch or did the interviews by conference phone call if they lived too far away to meet personally. Below is our interview script, but we also asked additional follow-up questions in light of what the interviewees shared.

1. Can we assume that you were once an associate staff member at a church? What positive qualities and practices did you experience with your supervisor that you have adopted in your own role as a supervisor of other staff members?
2. Supervising others in ministry includes two main aspects:

   - *supervision* to ensure that the job is being done well, and
   - *support* to ensure the well-being of those doing the work.

   What aspects of your role do you find come pretty naturally to you, and which are more challenging, or you have to be more intentional to ensure they are carried out well?
3. What have you found to be most helpful in your role as *supervisor,* ensuring that the job your associate staff members are doing is done well? Why do you think this has been so helpful?

4. What have you found to be most helpful in your role as *supporter*, promoting the well-being of those you supervise? Why do you think this has been so helpful?

5. Besides your own experience as an associate staff member, what else has prepared you for your current role as a ministry supervisor? What have you found helpful to grow and develop in this role?

6. One of the challenges of supervision is to know how to give increasing freedom to associate staff in their areas of ministry as they grow into their leadership roles. How have you adapted your supervision practices with your associate staff as they have grown on the job?

7. What kinds of things have you done to promote good/close relationships with those you supervise? How do you see this impacting the ways that you work together?

8. If you could change one aspect of your current supervision efforts with your associate staff, what would that be? Or, is there something you have wanted to do with your staff but have not figured out how to pull it off?

9. What do you do to help your church lay leaders (elders, deacons, overseers) support and encourage the church staff? How do you think supervising pastors can help create a supportive community and climate for the associate staff?

10. Is there anything else about supervising others in ministry that you think is important that we have not yet discussed? What else do you see as important?

Over the course of the interview process, we listened carefully to see what themes and practices could be identified, and what new things we were hearing from each supervising pastor. Toward the end of our data collection we noted the clear repetition of major themes and could no longer identify new themes or practices in what we were hearing. We determined that we had reached what qualitative researchers call "theoretical saturation."

Each of the interviews was recorded, and transcripts were created, allowing us to read back through what we had heard so we could code the themes and subthemes that emerged from the data. We also read back through the associate staff survey responses to note the themes that emerged there and how they related to what we heard in the interviews with the ministry supervisors. We then met (over breakfast, as usual) and discussed the major topics and themes we had identified and used that to help structure the chapters of this book and the topics addressed in each chapter. In the book, as much as possible, we use key quotes from the associate staff survey and the supervisor interviews to illustrate the issues and practices we write about. What you read in this book is our best effort to pass along to you what we have learned from those who serve as supervisors of other church staff members, and who do it well.

Notes

2. FORMING AND LEADING
THE MINISTRY TEAM

1. Portions of this chapter are adapted from a coauthored article: Kevin E. Lawson and Orbelina Eguizabal, "Leading Ministry Teams, Part II: Research on Effective Teams with Implications for Ministry Team Leadership," *Christian Education Journal* 6 (2009), pp. 265–81.

2. Ron R. Katzenbach and Douglas K. Smith, *The Wisdom of Teams*, Brighton, MA: Harvard Business Press, 1992, p. 45.

3. Ron R. Katzenbach and Douglas K. Smith, *The Discipline of Teams*, Hoboken, NJ: Wiley, 2001, p. 3.

4. Carl Larson and Frank LaFasto, *Teamwork: What Must Go Right, What Can Go Wrong*, Newbury Park, CA: Sage, 1989, p. 27.

5. Frank LaFasto and Carl Larson, *When Teams Work Best*, Newbury Park, CA: Sage, 2001, pp. 97–156.

3. TIME TOGETHER, PART I

1. My apologies to Charles Dickens fans for twisting his opening to *A Tale of Two Cities*.

4. TIME TOGETHER, PART II

1. P. Hersey and K. H. Blanchard, *Management of Organizational Behavior: Utilizing Human Resources*, Upper Saddle River, NJ: Prentice Hall, 1969. The "Life Cycle Theory of Leadership" was changed to the "Situational Leadership Model" in the third edition of the text, which came out in 1977.

5. FACILITATING AND SUPPORTING THE MINISTRY OF YOUR ASSOCIATE STAFF

1. Carl Larson and Frank LaFasto, *Teamwork: What Must Go Right, What Can Go Wrong*, Newbury Park, CA: Sage, 1989, pp. 109–11.

7. STAFF REVIEW AND DEVELOPMENT

1. John Maxwell, *The 21 Irrefutable Laws of Leadership*, Nashville: Thomas Nelson, 1998.

8. LETTING GO—STAFF TRANSITIONS

1. Lisa Cannon Green, "Despite Stresses, Few Pastors Give Up on Ministry," www.lifeway.com, Article URL: http://lifewayresearch.com/2015/09/01/despite-stresses-few-pastors-give-up-on-ministry/.
2. Ibid.
3. Michael Anthony and Mick Boersma, *Moving On Moving Forward: A Guide for Pastors in Transition*, Zondervan, 2007, see appendix.
4. Marshall Shelley and Dean Merrill, "The Pastor's Passages," *Leadership Journal* 4 (Fall 1983), p. 14.

9. SELF-CARE AS A MINISTRY SUPERVISOR

1. Lee Eclov, *Pastoral Graces*, Chicago: Moody Publishers, 2012, p. 11.
2. Ibid., p. 15.

Index

About the Authors

Mick Boersma served for four years in various associate pastor roles in Southern California, and as a senior pastor in Washington state for eleven years. He is professor of Christian Ministry & Leadership, director of Field Education and Placement, and chaplain at Talbot School of Theology. Mick and his wife, Rolane, launched a ministry to Talbot alumni in 1991, and continue to encourage women and men serving Christ around the world. He is active in his local church as a lead teacher in an adult fellowship. Mick is also coauthor of *Moving On Moving Forward: A Guide for Pastors in Transition* (Zondervan, 2007).

Kevin E. Lawson served on church staff for eleven years before moving to seminary teaching in the area of educational ministry. For over seventeen years, he served as director of the PhD and EdD programs in Educational Studies at Talbot School of Theology, in La Mirada, California. He is currently professor of Christian Education, teaching in these doctoral programs, and he remains active in his local church teaching adult Bible studies and has served as chairman of his church's elder board. He and Mick coauthored *Associate Staff Ministry: Thriving Personally, Professionally, and Relationally* (Rowman & Littlefield, 2014). They have also shared ownership in a blue 1963 Volkswagen Beetle, with Mick owning it from 1965–1997, and Kevin since 1997.

This book has addressed a number of ideas for supervising and supporting associate staff members. If you have ideas you would like to share with us, we'd love to hear from you, and invite you to send us an e-mail: mick.boersma@biola.edu or kevin.lawson@biola.edu.